THE PRNDL PROCESS

by Carl Brown

DEDICATION

For Mary

ITINERARY

INTRODUCTION

This book is based on actual events in my life. Most situations in this book represent amalgamations of experiences I've had. Some details differ from actual events or specific people in order to keep the story moving along and easier to read. Most names have been changed out of respect for privacy.

Is the PRNDL Process relevant ?

For over 100 years, advertisers and marketers have used the AIDA model. "AIDA" is an acronym that stands for Attention, Interest, Desire, and Action. This model has been used in settings where the sales/marketing/advertising message must first interrupt the prospect. Whether on TV, radio, or magazines, this model can be found everywhere.

But with advancements in technology and the globalized marketplace, it's easier to connect with niches who are already interested, have desires, and are willing to take action.

So, it should be easier to sell, right? Yes, but the globalized marketplace multiplies competition, and through technology, your prospects can compare you to your competition and abandon you with the click of a button or the swipe of a finger.

The challenge for us in the 21st century is to beat our competition in persuading, influencing, convincing, and calling to action the audience that is already interested.

So, instead of focusing on bringing your prospects through these broad phases of attention, interest, desire, and action, I recommend scripting a conversation or message with motives that resonate with the prospect. This scripting sequence is the PRNDL Process. (PRNDL stands for Park-Reverse-Neutral-Drive-Low, taken from automatic transmission gear selector. In this context, I use each of those steps as part of a process that will be explained further in the book.)

In order to understand the PRNDL Process, consider this

question, "Would you prefer to take the same vacation every year, or would you rather have something new and different every year?" You can't have both, can you? It's an either/or question. Some people are up for an adventure while others want their vacation carefully planned out. Some people are motivated by opportunity; others are motivated by minimizing risk. Some are motivated to save money, but for others, the prestige and quality that come with a high price tag are more important.

When we look closely, these examples show contradictory motivations. If some prospects want to minimize risk, they don't want to capitalize on an opportunity. If some prospects want to save money, then they are not looking for security at a higher price.

The PRNDL Process calls people to action by touching motivations that appeal to the broadest possible audiences. That brings us to the next question…

Is the PRNDL Process effective?

Some motivations are universally effective, or as close to universal as possible.

The PRNDL Process uses universal motivations, arranges them in an effective sequence, and uses a mnemonic device to make it easy to remember and implement.

We've established that not everyone is motivated to save money on every purchase. But almost everyone responds to an act of kindness, a favor, or a proper compliment. Responding well to this behavior is called "reciprocity." Since more people are motivated to reciprocate these messages, we should look for ways to induce reciprocity in our messaging. This motivation of reciprocity becomes the "R" in the PRNDL Process.

Is the PRNDL Process all you need?

No. The PRNDL Process is a template for scripting a message or sales script.

The broader sales process consists of several steps including:

1.) Market Research
2.) Prospect Research
3.) Qualify Prospects
4.) Build Rapport
5.) Identify the Problem
6.) Create Interest
7.) Present a Solution
8.) Justify the Purchase
9.) Close the Sale
10.) Follow-up

The PRNDL Process is intended to help you progress through these steps **after** you have arrived at Step 4.

But, no, the PRNDL Process is not all that you need. Body language, inflection, and presentation skills are all other topics that are worth mastering, and you can learn more about all of these on my website: http://www.PRNDLProcess.com

Is the PRNDL Process simple?

This book takes five broad universal motivations and arranges them in a sequence that can be used in scripting and in sales.

Is it really that easy? Five simple steps?

No. Sales is complicated and challenging.

To be great in sales, you must:

- Create a sense of urgency while not appearing pushy
- Find opportunities everywhere while not getting discouraged when they don't always happen
- Build relationships with anyone while not getting too personally invested in them
- Understand your prospect's budget while not spending other people's money
- Stay motivated while not getting discouraged by rejection

- Understand your competitor's features while believing in the advantages of your solution
- Find ways to close every sale while not exasperating your company's fulfillment staff
- Be flexible while staying focused

I've gone through sales training. I've read books on sales. I've trained, managed and coached a sales staff. Through all that, I realized things can really get complicated. Sales doesn't have to be complicated. Now that this book is published, I could write two more books about sales, but why complicate things? Let's keep it simple.

I was driving to work one day as I was going over my ideas about the sales process. "How can I simplify what I'm trying to teach?" I asked myself. I started thinking about different acronyms and phrases and mnemonics when I looked at the dashboard of my car and there it was: PRNDL.

That's it! It's easy to remember, everyone knows what the letters stand for, and it's in the right sequence.

> P- Park
> R-Reverse
> N- Neutral
> D-Drive
> L-Low

I've written the story of how I learned to sell in a way that teaches the elements of the PRNDL Process.

The PRNDL process gave me a mnemonic that's easy to remember, a sequence for messaging, and a metaphor for sales. The metaphor is getting your prospect to the destination that you recommend.

There are lots of different types of positions in sales (order takers, prospectors, qualifiers, hunters, fishers, etc.). With this metaphor, you could be a car salesman, a travel agent, a taxicab driver, a bus driver, or a street car racer. But in all cases, you want to get the prospect to the destination you recommend.

When it comes to the prospect, we want to get them in the right vehicle, drive on the route we recommend, give them directions, and see them through to the destination.

The metaphor applies in a different way to you as the sales person. You want to make sure you are in the right vehicle, with a properly tuned engine, using the right fuel, driving at the right speed, and taking the best route.

Will the PRNDL Process work for you?

In 2007, I read The Success Principle by Jack Canfield and I completed the "Life Purpose Exercise." On page 23 of my copy of the book I wrote, "My purpose is to use my enthusiasm and determination to inspire and properly form others to use their talents to reach their potential."

Since you're reading this book, you are helping me achieve my mission.

So, let me ask you to make yourself a promise. Finish this book and put these principles to work. Why would you start to read this book for any other reason? You'd be wasting your time!

Promise yourself right now that you will finish reading this book and that you will do the exercises in each chapter. Only when you do that can you answer the question, "Will the PRNDL Process work for me?"

1. START YOUR ENGINES

Road Map — What We'll Learn in This Chapter
- Winners land on their feet.
- Fish don't complain about being wet.
- We determine our own income levels.
- You must have RFW's to succeed.

The windshield wipers swayed back and forth. A disturbing, but necessary scraping, sliding sound came every three-seconds. Just enough of the falling snow was moved out of the way to reveal the tire tracks in the road as slushy, sloppy, soiled snow sprayed onto the curb. In the Midwest, a light snow can slow people down a bit, but this was enough to drop the average speed limit by 15 to 20 miles per hour.

The turn signal from the car in front of me glowed in intervals through 3 inches of unremoved snow. Then, the car slowly pulled out of my way. The V6 engine in my 1987 Buick Century could really get moving on a clear day. But in half a foot of snow, it moved at the same pace as my grandmother on a Sunday afternoon.

Chapter One – Start Your Engines

As I turned off the engine and stepped out of my car with rubber shoe protectors onto the snowy parking lot, I wondered why I had to park so far away from the building where I worked? Had it been a clear summer day, I wouldn't have cared. But the grey and dreary day invited dreams of being somewhere else, even if it was another job.

The door shut behind me as I walked past a row of grey office dividers. Okay, they were cubicles. But they only served to divide. Even though they doubled the possible work space in a building from the 1890s, they also blocked out all the beauty. They didn't provide privacy so much as they created a sense of imprisonment.

"Good morning," I said to a colleague with a fresh cup of coffee in his hand.

"Ehhh," he sighed. That was about all the excitement we got on a Monday morning, and the mood was as stale as the donuts leftover from Friday.

I hung up my trench coat, the obligatory attire of someone trying to be respectable on a university campus, even if I wasn't tenured. Okay, I wasn't even a professor, but the trench coat made me feel like a professional. I snapped the rubber shoe protectors off and splashed some melting slush on to the base of the coat tree. I turned on the computer and sat down to work.

Background

I worked hard. I liked to work. But in this environment, there was little to excite me.

We raised money for the university. It could have been exciting, if I had believed in the university. But what made this place different from any other place? If I ever thought it was special, I had long forgotten. And whether I worked hard or not, whether we reached our goals or not, whether everyone got along or not, everyone would get the same 3% cost-of-living salary increase. Not very exciting.

That pitiful increase just hurt more and more each year. Now that we had three kids, I had to start thinking of how to make more money. After eight years, I had already been promoted twice. Those promotions helped me to leapfrog over the paltry 3% increase, but my income was not where I wanted it to be. Let's face it, my income wasn't where I needed it to be. And for some reason, I had started setting an arbitrary goal of a six-figure income.

If you had told me that one day I would be a salesperson, I would never have believed it. I never really considered sales, and looking back I don't know why. Maybe it's because of a negative association with sales. Maybe because without the context of an industry, sales on its own doesn't mean anything. Selling cars is different from selling complicated engineering software. It's just that when you're selling complicated engineering software, you say you're in engineering. You don't say you're in sales.

There's nothing wrong with sales. And there's nothing wrong with car salesmen. It's just that so few people want to go into sales. But that's one of the great things about sales. Since so few people want to do it, it pays more. It's just the law of supply and demand. No matter what industry you're talking about, it's the sales person that makes the most — more than doctors, lawyers, or engineers.

After all, sales is just persuasion or influence, and the biggest reward goes to the person who has the greatest influence.

Nah! The company owner makes more than anyone, you might say. But the company owner has the primary sales position at the company. The owner has to sell the bank on the idea of future earnings. The owner has to sell the employees on the dream of working hard. The owner has to sell the customers products and services. The owner is always selling.

If there is a stigma against sales people, there shouldn't be. Nothing happens until something is sold. And let's face it, everybody is in the business of sales. Try interviewing someone for a sales position. Whether they want the job or not, they'll be in full sales mode. Whether they can do the job or not, they will quickly become a sales person. Either they'll tell you, "I could never do sales," or they'll tell you, "I could sell ice to an Eskimo."

Which, by the way, I've heard that line so many times. As if I'm supposed to be impressed? Eskimos make houses out of ice! They need ice. They use ice. Is it supposed to be hard to sell ice to an Eskimo? But in an interview for a sales position, everyone suddenly becomes a sales person because they immediately start selling to you. Either they're trying to convince you that they can sell, or they'll try to convince you they can't sell. But everyone is in the business of persuasion. Everyone is a sales person.

This is the story of how I learned to sell.

Winners Land on Their Feet

At that time, in this job at the university, we were in a hiring freeze. Our enrollment numbers were off by enough that the university budget was feeling a $1 million pinch. As a consequence, there were going to be no salary increases, no new hires, some early retirements, and every office had to find ways to save 10% in operating expenses. So, my chances of making six figures became even more unlikely.

As one o'clock rolled around that snow-laden day, we all started heading for the large conference room. The entire fund-raising arm at the university was an interesting group. Fundraising staff who solicit gifts were called "development officers," and they dressed the part— men in suits, ladies in business attire. The laptop was another dead giveaway. Support staff maybe had monochrome computer monitors while the development officers complained about how slow dial-up access was in airports and hotels. This was before you could find Wi-Fi at every restaurant and coffee shop.

I was a part of the support staff. But at least I wore a tie. Some of the guys who made up the group of "enlisted men," wore collared shirts but no ties. The difference in the two groups was striking. Why was I in this group? I knew the fundraisers made more money. After all, they were the sales people. Why couldn't I be in that group? Don't get me wrong; I didn't envy them in the bad sense of the word. My view is not that they didn't deserve it. Rather, I wanted to know what I had to do to earn six figures.

Our Vice President, Terri Landry greeted everyone from behind her podium. "Welcome everyone. It's good to see y'all." Her southern charm didn't overcome her subtle intimidation. "Come on in. Don't be shy. I don't bite."

Some people were afraid of her. A successful, smart professional from the deep South, Terri was leading us in an ambitious fundraising campaign. She'd run a successful campaign at another school in the South, and she must've been expensive to bring here.

"I want to take the time today to answer questions y'all have but maybe were afraid to ask. So, as you know, I asked my assistant, Barbara, to set up a way for everyone to ask questions anonymously if needed." Barbara was one of the friendliest people I've ever met, and the perfect go-between to put people at ease.

"And when I looked at y'all's questions, one thing came through very clear—FEAR." She cut to the chase and seized everyone's attention.

"I can tell that the hiring freeze and cost-cutting have some of y'all worried. But actually, you shouldn't be."

That was odd. "Actually." What does that mean? I tucked the question in the back of my mind.

"This is one of the most exciting times ever to be working at the university." Now I was wondering if we were speaking candidly or if this was all just baloney.

Terri went on to answer some innocuous questions that didn't have anything to do with anything. But she could smile and talk positively about everything. She started to deal with questions about operations and workflow. Questions about turf and ego. I didn't care about any of that. All I wanted to know was, how could I make six figures?

"Now, here is an example of what I think is a tough question." She paused and looked around the room. A couple of people leaned forward ever so slightly. "Do you make more than $100,000?"

Chapter One – Start Your Engines

She looked up from her notes at dozens of faces. It was so quiet that when the heating unit turned on and the blowers kicked in, everyone heard it. That's all we heard. Silence. Or hot air.

Maybe in some companies people know what everyone else makes. But not here. One of my former duties was to coordinate the budget, so I knew exactly how much everyone made— except her. Now, if she answered this question I would know it, and everyone else would too.

Terri broke the silence, "You know, actually, I was talking to the head of HR, and she said that the list of people at the university that make six figures is pages and pages long."

There it was again, "actually."

And now we all knew she made six figures. She never said it directly, but it was implied. I think that was part of her Southern charm and style. She implied things softly instead of answering sharply. I don't really remember much else from the rest of the meeting; just how I felt.

I was left with an empty feeling. I didn't have any excitement about what I did. And having a six-figure income here was obviously a possibility— just not for me.

It wasn't this instance of the word "actually" that turned me off completely. But in this case I was left with a bad taste in my mouth. It took me several more years, but eventually I learned that the word is only used when someone is in full-blown sales mode— trying to sell you something against your better judgement. Now, whenever someone uses it, red flags go up in my mind. And I strongly discourage anyone from using that word in any sales script. I'll explain more in chapter four.

As I walked out of the meeting, my path crossed with a fund-raising co worker I respected. "So, Carl," she said disarmingly. "What did you think about that?" Friendly, but straight to the point.

"Well, it didn't fill me with hope."

"Me neither," she sighed.

"What are you going to do?" I asked.

"The same thing happened at the bank when I worked there. Back when I used to take the number 5 bus into downtown every day. There was a time when morale was really low." She emphasized the words, "really low" as she turned and looked me right in the eye. "We had a job freeze. People were getting laid off."

I held the door for her and then caught back up with her as we left the building. "But, winners land on their feet." She continued, "I landed on my feet then, and I'm going to land on my feet now."

Immediately, I knew two things. (1) I was a winner, and (2) I would land on my feet.

I just didn't know how or where I would land.

Planting a Seed

When I got home after work, it was my turn to give my wife a break. I would come home, she would go work out and get some quiet time to think. She's a great mom and she deserves a chance to spend part of her day by herself. We had three kids, and she was homeschooling the oldest two. I tried to help out when I could. Science Saturday. Spanish with Dad. Whatever I could do.

Maybe I would make dinner, or maybe she would have it ready, but this was my chance to spend time with my kids. I love my kids. I loved playing with them, reading to them, feeding the toddler, and I made up my mind early on that I wouldn't complain about changing diapers. I love being a Dad.

I had just spent time wrestling with my kids and tossing them onto couch cushions, having a blast, when my brother called.

"What's up, Daniel?" I asked.

Daniel is my younger brother, and he had recently been looking for a new job when I connected him with a friend of mine from the homeschooling group. His name was Doug and he was selling insurance. And apparently he was growing the business, or he was in human resources, because I knew he was filling a couple of spots when I suggested they get together.

"How are things going with Doug?"

"Aw, man, things are crazy! Thanks for introducing us. I never knew how big the insurance industry is."

Daniel was an introvert, but his energy was coming through the phone receiver loud and clear.

"Seriously?" I asked. "What do you mean?"

"Man, they have agents all over the country. This business is growing. It's huge! We're set to double in the next six months!"

"Wow. Sounds serious."

"It is! We had a meeting of all the agents in the area last night, and there's this girl who basically said she just goes out and picks up checks from people."

"What do you mean?" I asked skeptically.

"We send out these letters to people who just financed a mortgage letting them know we can help them get mortgage protection to cover the loan if they die, so their family doesn't lose the house."

"Right. Life insurance, right? Amy and I refinanced about six months ago, and we got policies for both of us."

"You did?" he sounded disappointed.

"Yeah, why?" I asked.

"Well, because I was going to get you signed up. Do you have enough coverage?"

I thought back to the guy who came to our house. Nice guy. We got a policy on Amy and one for me. They also had some coverage in case the kids died. It made a lot of sense.

"Yeah, I have enough," I shared.

"Well, do you know anyone else who needs coverage?" he laughed.

"I don't know." I hesitated.

"So, the other thing you could do, Carl, is…" He paused. "You could sell insurance," he switched topics.

"Why would I want to do that?" I asked.

"Well, are you happy with your salary at the university?"

"Well… no. Not really."

"How much would you like to make," he asked.

I wasn't sure how long I wanted this conversation to keep going, so I gave him an answer that should have put him off quickly. "Man, I need to make six figures."

"You can make six figures with us."

Silence.

"Seriously?" I finally responded.

"Yup. Lots of guys do. We have a conference call every week and they read out the names of the leaderboards… that's who turned in the most business for the week. There's a bunch of new people who are going to make six figures this year."

Wow. I was seriously impressed.

"And there's no limit. You can make way more than $100,000. There's guys on track to make 2, 3 and even $400,000. The bottom line, Carl, is that you can't really get ahead by trading time for money."

One of the kids fell down and was crying for me. And I was ready to get off the phone anyway.

"You'll have to tell me more about it sometime," I pretended not to be interested. "Good luck."

"Okay, good-bye."

My kid brother had landed on his feet. I was happy for him. At the same time, I was intrigued by what he was doing.

I thought a lot more about the idea of trading time for money. Though I didn't fully comprehend it at that point, I could see that trading time for money was a trap. In order to get beyond paying my bills, I would need to trade value for money and the best way to do that seemed to be a career in sales.

Fish Don't Complain About Being Wet

Several days later, around lunch time I drove to a nearby neighborhood and pulled out a bag lunch. I enjoyed a talk-radio program at noon, and I found that the best way to enjoy lunch was driving around for an hour. Nothing felt as liberating as eating what I wanted, when I wanted, where I wanted, doing what I wanted. Looking back, it wasn't the best use of time or money, but I learned one of the greatest lessons of my professional career that day.

"It's just so frustrating," complained the guest caller.

"All right," the radio show host paused. I had tuned in during the middle of a conversation. I perked up as I tried to make up for not knowing what the conversation was about. "Now let me ask you a question. You're frustrated with your customers?"

"Yes!" he answered emphatically.

"You're frustrated with the way your business is being impacted by the global economy and the development of technology?"

"Yes," he answered cautiously. I wondered where he was going with this line of questioning.

"So my question is... Didn't you choose this business?"

"Yes," the caller answered, "I love doing this."

"You just don't like the circumstances or the environment you're in?"

"No. No, I don't."

"Well, why don't you get out of that business? Why complain about it? You know, fish don't complain about it being wet."

Then the host addressed his audience, "Folks, we can choose what we do. If we complain about it, we choose it all the more. In this economy, in this day and age, if you are stuck somewhere, chances are you can change it. Never before in the history of the world have there been so many lateral job changes. If you choose not to leave the job you're in, then you're choosing the job you're in."

He went on. "We can only control the things we can control. We all have 24 hours in a day. So, how can some people not have enough time? Does anyone have more time than anyone else? To complain about your circumstances is to admit you are powerless over them. People have made fortunes who started with nothing. If they had more drive than you do, is that their fault? If they could change their circumstances, are they just smarter? Harder working? If you want to change your circumstances, you can change them! But if all you are going to do is complain about your circumstances, then you are admitting defeat."

He was on a roll. "We choose what industry we get in, what business model we get in, what job level we enter, what hours we work, what profit margin there is, how many vacation days there are. My advice to you? Go where the money is! Even in a depression, money still gets spent. We can choose to stay in a dead-end job or a dying industry. Or we can choose to take responsibility for our lives. Stack the deck in your own favor. Go where the money is! Get a job in an industry that has a future! But once you choose your job, your business, your industry, don't complain about it. Do something about it!"

This type of message doesn't show up in the news, but I found this short segment on talk radio in the middle of the day to be very inspiring. Ultimately it is me who is responsible for my life. If I didn't like where I worked, there wasn't anything that anybody else could do about it but me. If I didn't like the industry I was in, there wasn't any use blaming anyone else.

This thought was in the back of my head for far too long before I finally did something about it. It was clear now that I couldn't complain about my circumstances. And I understood that I was the one who could determine my own income.

Looking back, I realized two things were missing. The first was an understanding of where I could go. And the second was a pressing need. I needed "RFW's," or "reasons for working."

Who Determines Your Income?

A few days later, after a quiet lunch in my car, I pulled back into the parking lot and headed for my boss' office. We had our regular weekly meeting scheduled, but I didn't know this meeting was going to change my perspective and my career.

There aren't too many interactions that I can say changed my career, but this was one of them.

In my meeting, I reviewed the progress I was making with an intern that I had hired. His name was Isaac, and he had one of the best attitudes I've ever encountered in the workplace. When I interviewed him, he didn't show a higher level of skill than other candidates. But he demonstrated confidence and determination that convinced me he would figure out what he needed in order to get the job done.

"And Isaac is graduating in June," I complained to my boss, in a dispirited, defeated, powerless kind of way. (I had not yet fully embraced the idea that fish don't complain about being wet.)

"What does he want to do?" she asked, appearing to make small talk.

"He wants to be a site manager for a construction company," I replied, not realizing she was trying to teach me something.

"What does a site manager make?" She asked.

Thinking we were making small talk, I replied with a half-hearted, "I dunno."

Then she said it. She revealed something profound. Something monumental. It's not every day when someone tells you something that you later realize is worth over $1 million of income to you.

She simply said, "Don't you think you had better find out?"

It may have taken me a minute to digest that. In fact, I might have missed her point completely for several days. But when it sunk in, that's what changed my career.

She was telling me that Isaac determined his own salary.

Let that sink in for a minute.

Let's suppose for a moment that Isaac had wanted to make, "a little more" than what he was making working for us. Let's suppose he wanted to be a $40,000 employee. Well, whatever he had decided already would likely become the amount we would offer him.

Some might say this is unfair. What if one intern was being paid $20,000 and Isaac got the same job making $40,000. Would this be unfair to the intern making $20,000 if that's what he agreed to? I don't know. That didn't happen, but it could have happened.

Some might say, "Well, maybe Isaac didn't determine what he's ultimately capable of making. He just determined what he would be offered for this job." If you think that, you might be right to a point. After all, Isaac could have dreamt about taking a company public and netting $2 billion. But we would not have hired him for $2 billion.

But for now, where he was, Isaac was determining his own income potential. And if he'd wanted to make $100,000 and had balanced that with a plan to deliver that much value, then I would have bet on Isaac.

Let's look at it another way. Suppose Isaac had no aspiration beyond his hourly wage. Then I would have wanted to keep him, and we would never have talked about it, so his pay would have continued at the hourly wage.

RFWs (Reasons For Working)

One night when I came home from work, Amy wasn't ready to go work out. Dinner wasn't ready.

"Want me to make pizza?" I asked. Pizza was my specialty. Sourdough crust. Thin, but sturdy crust. Pepperoni with the edges just beginning to brown. Cornmeal dusting to prevent the pizza from sticking to the pan. Mmmmm.

"Sure," she said. Something seemed off.

"Do we have any pizza sauce?" I asked, rummaging through the pantry.

"I don't know."

"I don't see any in here. Did you go shopping?"

Amy was already walking upstairs, and I could tell something was wrong. I followed her upstairs.

"I can't go shopping. I don't even have a grocery list made," she sounded defeated.

"Okay," I replied. "Want me to go shopping?"

"I can't make a grocery list, Carl. I don't understand what's wrong."
It took us 10 years to find a doctor who put all the pieces together, and that's a story for another time. Needless to say, we were not going to be able to continue homeschooling.

Amy and I loved homeschooling. It was great for our family. It was great for our kids. We had many friends who homeschooled and it was our community. But now we were facing the prospect of not being able to homeschool.

The only real solution as we saw it was private school. But I didn't make nearly enough money to send our kids to private school. This was the impetus for me to put several thoughts together.

Winners land on their feet.
Trading time for money can be a trap.
Fish don't complain about being wet.
We determine our own income levels.
I had RFW's.

So when Daniel called me again, it was easier for me to be open to the idea of selling insurance with him.

Another Seed is Planted
"Why don't you come with me to this conference next weekend?" Daniel asked.

"But I have to take off work, and pay for an airline ticket."

"Right," he said, "But the only reason I'm telling you this is because you're looking to make six figures, right?" He was right. Nothing changes until something changes. "And listen. Doug made over $100,000 two years ago, and he made over $200,000 last year!"

"That's amazing!" I said, almost in disbelief.

Imagine making six figures! That was almost double what I was making. And if Doug can do it, then I knew I could too.

"All right, I'm in!" I said.

The next couple of days, I couldn't wait to go to this conference.

Rear View Mirror — What We Learned in Chapter One
- Winners land on their feet.
- Trading time for money can be a trap.
- Fish don't complain about being wet.
- We determine our own income levels.
- We must have RFW's to succeed.

Chapter One Exercises

1. What goal do you have right now? ***Write this down before going on to the next chapter.***

My Goal(s):

_____

_____

_____

2. What aspects of your work do you complain about, but have the ability to change in the long-term?

_____

_____

_____

3. List your "reasons for work".

_____

_____

_____

4. Make a resolution to stop complaining about things out of your control, and to do something about things you **can** control.

2. GET OUT OF PARK!

Road Map — What We'll Learn in This Chapter
- You can't steer a parked car.
- How to leverage past behavior of a prospect in order to develop rapport.

The Sales Conference

Music was blasting from the conference room at the hotel like a fraternity party. As we got closer, there were swarms of people coming from the parking lot, the elevators, and from the other side of the building.

We walked into the conference room. People were on their feet in rows of chairs and clapping in a beat synchronized to the music.

"This is going to get exciting," Doug winked at me as though I was going to be awarded a trophy.

I was a little skeptical at first, but it was hard not to get caught up in the swell of excitement.

"Who's ready?" asked the man on the stage.

"We are," responded a chorus of people in the crowd.

"Ya coulda fooled me," the man on stage wasn't convinced.

"Who's that?" I asked my brother.

"That's Randy."

"That's the guy?" I asked. He's not like what I pictured. Daniel and Doug had told me about him. This guy was the brains behind everything. On stage, he seemed a little informal. He challenged my expectations of what a successful business owner looked like and acted.

Randy wore a broad frame and an even broader smile as he cupped his hands to his ears and asked the crowd again, "I say, who's ready to git started?"

More voices joined in this time, "We are!"

"I can't hear ya. I say, who's ready?"

"WE ARE!" This guy obviously knew how to work a crowd.

"BOOM YEAH!" he yelled, satisfied that they were ready.

"BOOM YEAH!" the crowd yelled back.

"I said, BOOM YEAH!" he yelled back.

It was hard not to laugh or get drawn in by the excitement.

"That's right. BOOM YEAH! Let's git this thang started." Randy's southern drawl created a unique spectacle. I didn't know whether to laugh at him or laugh with him.

"BOOM YEAH!" It seemed like it never got old.

After whipping the crowd into a frenzy, he calmed everyone down by showing charts and graphs demonstrating the impressive growth of the group.

"We submitted 25,000 applications last week which put us over the top for 100,000 for the month." The crowd cheered.

My brother leaned over to me, "That's exactly what he predicted last year."

"And if ya look at this chart, you'll see that the annual premium is going up, too. Seems like there's a correlation between the number of applications we submit and the annual premium."

The crowd laughed at anything he said that sounded remotely like a joke. There was one woman in particular in the front row that just found Randy to be hysterical. And when she laughed at his jokes, it was contagious. On the one hand, he was simple, funny, and charismatic. On the other hand, he was accurate in his projections, and he seemed to know his business very well.

"Three years ago, people were saying it couldn't be done, but we did it. YOU did it!"

The crowd loved it.

"Now, if we are submitting 100,000 a month, that means that we're on track to hit two million by the end of next year. And what that means is that there are bunches, and I mean bunches, of new folks out there who are going to earn a six-figure income."

My ears perked up.

Normally I'm a skeptic. But he just showed us how his business had grown dramatically over the past three years. And he had a room full of people who sure seemed motivated to go out and increase the numbers even more. What really impressed me was when he asked six new Agency Managers to come up to the stage. As Agency Managers, they had recruited enough agents to have their own agency. I didn't know what exactly what that meant, but these six people were now on track to make $100,000 and the crowd was cheering them on.

"Okay, what about you, Bryan? How long have you been here?" Randy asked the first guy.

It was this first guy that blew me away. "I got in this morning," he said nervously.

Everyone laughed.

"Naw, I mean how long have you been with us?" Randy clarified.

"Oh, oh, right," he stammered. "It's been almost two years."

"And how much business did your agency turn in last week?" Randy asked.

"Umm. Let's see. Umm." This guy was nervous. "I think it was, about. Umm."

Neither of them were behind a podium, so I could see both of them completely. And this guy, Bryan, was so nervous that his knees were shaking up and down. I had never seen anyone's knees shake before. There were times when my knees shook, but I had never seen someone else's knees shake.

"Go on. Take your time," Randy consoled him.

"We were. Umm. I was. Umm." The crowd started to snicker and it distracted him. "I'm sorry. What was the question? I'm a bit nervous."

This was unbelievable. This guy was nervous standing in front of the group, even though he had just hit an important milestone. I don't know how to express what I was going through right then. I always had a level of self-confidence, but when I saw that this guy could be successful with apparently much less confidence, I reasoned that I, too, could be successful.

The Script

After the excitement had died down a bit, Randy had another guy come out to share the specifics of "the sale." Now, as you're reading this book, I don't imagine that you'd be interested in reading a sales script for something you may never sell.

But I want to share this script with you, because of how simple it is. And besides, it's nowhere near technical.

Not only is it simple, but looking back, I realize how effective it was. We weren't taught the psychological components of this script, because there was no need to complicate things. Throughout the rest of this story, you'll see how the elements of this script can be broken down and re-engineered to fit just about any business, industry, product, or service.

Here is the script in its simplest form:

- Is this the letter you sent into us?
- Okay, well, I assume that you care about each other and that you want to make sure that if anything happens to either of you, that you won't lose your house. Is that right?
- Okay, so, what was it about this letter that made you send it in to us?
- Now, I can't get you approved for this coverage.
- What I can do is explain how this coverage works, then we can submit an application with the first month's premium to see if we can get it approved.
- Does that make sense?
- {After you explain the coverage, you take the application and with a pen in your hand, you say:}
- You don't know your driver's license number, do you?

That's it. That's the script.

Once I saw that someone like Bryan could do it, and when I saw how simple the script was, I was ready to do this full-time.

During the break, I was talking with Daniel about what we had seen and heard.

"So, you think you can do this?" he asked me.

"Absolutely!"

"So, how many leads do you want to get started with?"

"I don't know, 10 or 15 maybe. That one guy on stage said you can't really manage more than 30 at a time."

"That's true," he agreed.

All this excitement was really getting to me. "I'll tell you what, Daniel, once I get started on calling those leads, you had better watch out because I'm going to be turning in more business than you!"

He laughed. Right then, Scott and Greg walked over to us. "Hey guys," he said to them, "Carl here was just telling me about what he's going to do when we get back from this conference. Why don't you tell them, Carl?"

I felt cornered. I had just been talking big about what I was going to do, and I believed it. And telling my brother I was going to outperform him was one thing, but I wasn't prepared to share my goals out loud with strangers.

"Go on. Tell them what you told me," he goaded me on.

Right there, I learned about the power of publicly stating your goals. Telling my brother was one thing, but telling strangers my goals was intimidating. But I'm glad he forced me to say it.

"I was just saying," my chest puffed up, "how Daniel here had better watch out because I'm going to be turning in more business than he is once we get back."

"Well, you guys will have to try and keep up with me," Scott answered back quickly.

"I'm not even worried about you losers," Greg added. "You guys can fight over who fills in the lower half of the leaderboard because I'm going to be at the top of the leaderboard, and you won't even come close."

The rivalry was good for everyone. Now, it was up to each of us to live up to our own standards.

You Can't Steer a Parked Car

After the break, some more heart-pounding music, and frenzied hysterics, the group reassembled in the conference room and sat down to listen to Randy talk about getting started as an agent. Apparently, Randy had run leads on mortgage protection for years before managing an agency and training agents across the country. Because there were a lot of new agents like me at this conference, we covered a lot of training.

"If you call one of these leads and they sound angry, just remember, it's not about you! They're upset about work. They're mad at their dog. Their kids left a mess in the living room. Whatever is going on in their life was going on way before you came along. But… But they sent us this letter!"

Randy added, "They got a mortgage and maybe it's their first mortgage, maybe it's their second. Either way, they decided it was important to protect the house they got. So, when they sent this letter in to us, they wanted to protect something important. Your job is to remind them about that. Reconnect them with the feelings they had when they sent in this letter. You're not starting from ground zero. When you call one of these names, you're not cold-calling. They have already warmed up to us. Your job is to rekindle that warmth and bring it to a boil."

This made a lot of sense and it made me comfortable with these leads. Randy was right. These people already sent us a letter. They started it. We can choose our industry and our business model and many of the circumstances in our lives. Why start with prospects who are at ground zero? Why not start with prospects who already want what you have?

There are many different metaphors that can be used to convey the psychology or mechanics of sales. But if we use the analogy of a journey or the metaphor of a car on a highway with directions to a destination, the key thing is to find people who want to go where you can take them.

Why bother trying to convince people about something they don't want? Why not start with people who are going where you want to take them?

Find the people already in route to your destination and walk alongside them. Speak their language. Talk about where they came from. Get them to tell you why they want to go where they're going. Then, when they tell you what's important to them, ask them why that's important to them. Then ask again and keep drilling down into what's really at the source of their motivation. Once they do that, they will have convinced themselves and you that they need what you have to offer.

"Is this the letter you sent into us? Okay, well, I assume that you care about each other and that you want to make sure that if anything happens to either of you, you won't lose your house. Is that right?"

Randy referenced the script again, and I could see the brilliant simplicity of it. Our job was to reconnect our prospects with the feeling they had when they sent that letter in to us. I must have started to day-dream, because when I tuned back in to what Randy was saying, he seemed to be on a tangent.

"The point I'm making is to get out in the field and get started. Then, when you make mistakes, call your Agency Manager and ask how to fix your mistakes. You can't steer a parked car, ladies and gentlemen. You have to get out on the road, meet with some people, make mistakes and then learn from your mistakes. Success is the result of Good Judgement, which is the result of Experience, which is the result of Bad Judgement. You can't learn how to walk without falling down once or twice."

After a pause, he continued, "Confidence comes from doing. So, get out there and do something and you'll get experience."

He had a lot of great one-liners, but the one that stuck with me was, "You can't steer a parked car." And even though he was talking about managing sales people, the concept was applicable to dealing with prospects.

Once a car is in motion, it's easier to steer it. Once a prospect is motivated, it's easy to steer them towards having our solution meet their needs. Once one of our new recruits got started, it would be easier to correct small points than to try to get someone started from nothing in sales.

My First Appointment

After attending the sales conference in Atlanta, I was convinced I could make my income goals. I still didn't know anything about insurance or about sales. I just knew I had to keep taking steps in the right direction.

After my workday was over, I studied for the insurance exam I needed to take in order to get an insurance license. During lunch hours, I dialed into conference calls for as much sales training as I could get.

After a couple weeks, I attended the state-required insurance school on the weekend. Then, I took a long lunch break one day and drove across town to take the insurance exam.

Finally, I was able to take some leads, call prospects, book appointments, and get started selling! One of my first appointments was quite a drive from my house. That day, I packed a lunch and a dinner. I left the office at the end of the day and ate dinner in the car as I drove to my first appointment.

The client had replied to a mailing asking for mortgage protection. They provided their name, height, weight, date of birth, and contact information. All of the details from the sales training were too much for me. If the client was over the age of 80, could they be insured? I didn't know. What medical conditions required an extra questionnaire to be added to the application? I didn't know. I was nervous, but I was anxious to get started. Truth be told, I was so eager and so irresponsible that I jumped right in. "Ready? Fire! Aim."

Joy opened the door after I knocked.

"Carl?" she asked.

"That's right. Are you Joy?"

"I am. Come on in. Would you like something to drink? Maybe water?"

"Yes, I would. Thank you."

Their house was modest, but tastefully decorated. From the style of furniture, the wallpaper, and the art on the wall, I could tell they started their family in the '70s.

She led me to the kitchen table where I met her husband, Roy. He sat across the table from me with his hands folded on the table in front of him. He wasn't intimidating in any way. His face was welcoming and he was ready to get down to business. Randy was right. We just needed to reconnect our prospects with the reason they sent this letter in to us.

I pulled out their letter and put it in front of them. They had seen this before. It was filled out in their own handwriting. It had their name, birthday, height, and weight on it.

"Is this the letter you sent in to us?" I asked, leaving an uncomfortably long period of silence lingering in the air. I could hear the ticking from the clock on their living room fireplace.

"Yes," Joy responded. She picked it up and looked at it.

I waited just a few more moments before I broke the silence. Tick, tick, tick.

"Now I assume that since you sent this letter in, you want to make sure that Joy here is taken care of, in case anything should happen to you."

Another lengthy pause.

Some more ticking of the clock.

They both quietly and slowly nodded.

"Is that right?" I asked after the empty silence had left its mark.

"Heck yes," he said.

"I mean, I don't even work," she said, "I raised the kids all those years. I don't have a job. And if anything happened to him, I'd lose the house."

"And we are just..." He paused. "Well, we had to drop that other policy, but when we saw this in the mail, we thought we should get that coverage back in place."

I worked through the script, filled out the application, and asked them to write out a check for the first month's premium.

"Who do we make it out to?" he asked.

Crap! I didn't know. I was dying of embarrassment on the inside. On the outside, I tried to be as cool as a cucumber.

"You know what?" I asked. "I don't know. Congratulations, you are my first clients! And I'm sorry, but I need to call my manager to ask him who to write the check out to."

"Wow," Joy was surprised. "We're your first clients?"

"Yes ma'am." I smiled somewhat nervously. "Congratulations!"

Facing the embarrassment head-on seemed like the best thing to do.

As I left the house with a completed application and a check for the first month's premium, I was so excited that I could hardly remember how to walk and dial the cell phone at the same time. But I called my brother. I had just been on the phone with him, so he was going to want to know how it went. Otherwise, I would have called Amy first.

"So you picked up a check?" he asked, like a kid asking about Christmas gifts.

"Yep," I said with more confidence than I remembered having in a long time.

"How much was it for?" he asked impatiently.

"OK, hold on," I said because I reached for the application.

"You don't remember? How could you not remember? They just wrote you the check a few minutes ago, right?"

"Yeah, I'm not even in my car yet," I laughed, "Man, I don't know it's all such a blur to me. I just... I don't know. For crying out loud, I didn't even know who they should write the check out to. "

I fumbled my car keys, the laptop bag and the application.

"It's 100 something. " I said nervously.

"Are you serious?" He asked.

"I think so. Hold on. Let me get in the car." I got in the car, turned on the dome light, and looked at the application, "$185."

"Monthly or quarterly?" He asked. "You didn't do it quarterly, did you?"

"Umm. No. $185 monthly."

"Carl, do you know how much money you just made?"

"No. Why?" I was fumbling with my map to find how to get out of the neighborhood. Math was not on my mind.

"$185 times 12 and 55% of that." I could hear him punching the numbers on his calculator, "That's $1,220 Carl!"

"Sweet! Are you serious?"

He was ecstatic. So was I.

"What did I tell you? This is where it's at."

If I could do that in one appointment, I could make this work. I can make six figures. I was on my way. That night I also picked up another check for $75 at a separate appointment. $75 times 12 is $900 of annual premium. And 55% of that is $495 commission. I had made over $1,700 in one night. Hopefully now I could quit my job and do this full-time.

So– how did I do it?

Well, maybe it was my advantage that I didn't know anything because I followed the script perfectly. Later, I would be cocky and think I could improvise, and that would reinforce the lesson– stick with what works. Stick with the script!

In this case, by responding to people who had already sent in a form saying they wanted mortgage protection, we were employing one of the biggest factors of influence. We were getting people to take small steps, then bigger steps, and bigger steps until they said 'Yes' to the whole thing.

"You can't steer a parked car," I remember Randy saying.

He was talking about training someone in sales. But the same principle applied here. This couple was not a parked car. They were already heading in the direction I wanted them to go. All I had to do was give them a little direction. And once a car is in motion, it's easier to steer it the way you want. But you cannot steer a parked car.

If I had begun my appointment without encouraging them and finding out why they needed this, I would have turned them off. The beauty of this first step is that we were there for their reasons. I just pulled alongside them and pointed out they were not in "Park."

Find out why your prospect is not in *"PARK"* and let them tell you why they need what you have.

The "Why"

The first step has been referred to as "the Why" or Congruency.

It's just using the momentum your prospect has created to help them be consistent. Your prospects have already taken steps towards buying from you. They have already created momentum in the direction of buying from you. They are not "in **PARK**." They are already in motion. That is congruency. A dictionary entry for congruence is "the quality or state of agreeing or corresponding."

When we behave in a manner consistent with our previous behavior, that is congruency. In other words, when we have congruency, we are acting in character. By contrast, when we do something unexpected or out of character, we are incongruent.

We all have patterns of behavior we exhibit. Those patterns become our personality. Once we have established patterns, we identify with that behavior, and we are motivated to continue those habits and patterns. Our job as people of influence, is to find proof that our prospects have taken small steps towards buying, and magnify those steps. Or we can create opportunities to get them to take steps towards buying.

Of the other 4 steps in the PRNDL process, this one is essential. You can't skip it. Without congruency, the sale may never happen. And sometimes, with enough congruency, you don't even need the other steps. Your prospects might have so much momentum built up that nothing can stop them.

One word of caution: Don't overplay this step.

"You don't want to railroad them," Randy said on the conference call one day. "A man convinced against his will is of the same opinion still."

It's also important to note that your prospects are going to have their own reasons for buying. And their reasons may be different from your reasons. In this case, Roy and Joy told me what their reason was. They told me what was important to them. All I had to do was explain how I could meet their needs.

The opposite of this is the stereotypical view of a salesman who wants to "Get his foot in the door."

THE PRNDL PROCESS

If your prospect has the door closed, there's not much value in sneaking your foot in. A closed door is a parked car. You might be able to sell to that type of person, but why waste your time? You'll end up getting pretty frustrated. There are already lots of people closer to the sale. Just find them and pull up alongside them.

This is what is meant by congruency. The best prospect is taking steps toward the purchase already. You just want to help them take more steps. Help them take bigger steps. Help them get closer and closer to making a purchase.

One time, I walked into a car dealership and I obviously wanted to buy a car. Some young and inexperienced salesman walked over and said, "Can I help you find something?" Not a bad start. I said, "Yes, I'm looking for a sedan."

His response blew me away. "Our V6 model has 280 horsepower with the direct injected 3.4 L engine, a direct injection fuel line, 110 inch wheelbase, 127 ft.^{3} interior and gets great gas mileage. Let me grab you one of our new brochures." I left as soon as he turned around.

The reality is I don't remember what he said, because I didn't understand it when he said it. I was like a parked car when he came along with a bulldozer to push me towards his recommendation.

So, the first step is to recognize that you can't steer a parked car. Once you realize that, you can identify why the prospect isn't in park. What direction are they heading? Why are they going that direction? How fast are they going? We want to help our prospects keep taking steps until the only thing left is for them to buy from us.

Rear View Mirror — What We Learned in Chapter Two
- We can't steer a parked car.
- Leverage past behavior and past choices of a prospect in order to develop rapport and build momentum.
- See the Appendix for examples of using the first part of The PRNDL Process: **PARK.**

Chapter Two Exercises
1. What goal do you have right now? *Copy your goal from Chapter One, or write a new goal.*

My Goals:

_____

_____

_____

2. Thinking back to previous sales you've closed, list some examples of how that prospect was no longer "in *PARK*" before you met them. What had they done to create momentum towards the sale? (i.e., they already use your product, they called you, they agreed to a meeting, etc.)

_____

_____

_____

_____

_____

3. From observation of previous sales, what can you do for or say to other prospects to create or build congruency in order to "steer" them towards a purchase? See the Appendix for examples of using the first part of The PRNDL Process: **PARK**.

_____

_____

_____

_____

_____

_____

4. From the examples above, brainstorm 3-5 things you can look for in prospecting to steer people who are not "parked cars."

_____

_____

_____

_____

_____

3. BELIEVE!

Road Map — What We'll Learn in This Chapter

- The way you look at the world determines everything.
- If you want to succeed, you must aim for excellence.
- Surround yourself with people who are going where you want to go.
- Success only comes from taking action.
- What an income thermometer and why you should have your income thermometer checked.
- If you agree to settle for less, then that's probably what you'll get.

Cleaning House

Footsteps in the hallway.

They weren't high heels. They weren't dress shoes.

They were accompanied by the sound of wheels being turned. Something was being pushed down the hall by someone.

When you sit in a cubicle, you get to the point where you can spot someone by the way they walk. Some people walk with a heavy pace, almost like they're stomping. Some people walk softly. Some people have long strides, some short. Some walk faster than others.

One woman in our building wore so much perfume that you could literally smell her coming. But these footsteps were unmistakable. It was Darryl the janitor, and he was coming to empty the trash.

"Can you believe what's been happening in D.C.?" Darryl tried to engage me in conversation.

I might have fallen for it on some other day. I enjoy talking about politics, but only from the standpoint that policy matters. I do not like talking about politics as a soap opera of never-ending indignation, speculation, intrigue, and slander.

"I think so, Darryl. But I'm not sure. What do you mean?" I lied.

There had been days where talking with Darryl would last a full 60 minutes. It had gotten well out of control. And I was at a point where I was already mentally checked out of this job and thinking about working leads.

I remember having the realization that senioritis is not just a condition that high school seniors have when they are ready to get out of high school. I had senioritis, and I wanted to get out of this job and go make sales.

Fortunately, Darryl was fairly predictable with his timing, and I could usually tell when he was close by. Since he didn't know what we did on a day-to-day basis, it wasn't rude when I continued typing on the computer a few moments after he walked up.

"Well, they are up to it again!" He started. "You have to admit one thing, Carl. Even you have to admit this..."

Ring! My phone interrupted.

"Oh, sorry Darryl, I better take this," I trailed off to a whisper.

Picking up the phone in a routine way, I answered, "Carl Brown."

"Who is your lifeline, Carl?" The other voice said.

"Oh, right! No, I don't have that done," I pretended. "I will get that back to you right away!"

I looked at Darryl, shrugged my shoulders and motioned with my eyes towards the phone in my hand. "Sorry," I whispered, but Darryl was already on his way to his next victim.

"Miss Sharon! How are you doing? Did you see the game this weekend?" For me, it was politics. For Sharon, it was sports.

Back to the phone, I kept up the charade, "OK. Are you gonna be there long?"

The voice came back, "OK Carl, I don't know how you get into these situations."

"Right. OK," I said. "I'll be there in a couple minutes."

"Well, I hope my call helped."

"Yes. Thanks. Bye." Whew! I was spared again.

Just about every day I e-mailed a friend across the hall and asked him to call me and save me from another waste of time.

Who managed Darryl? Did they realize he spent all his time talking to people? How many trash cans can you empty if you talk to everyone for five minutes?

It's not that I didn't like Darryl, but I had to prioritize. If I wasn't careful, I would end up talking with him for one hour every day.

Interoffice communications require a delicate balancing act.

At the sales convention, Randy had a similar message about wasting time with the prospect. "If you're going to have pie, you should have pie with your wife at home. You don't have time to socialize on the road. Be friendly, but don't make friends with your clients."

Chapter Three – Believe!

I kept up the charade, got my notebook, and headed to the office of our Vice President. Terri was friendly and gracious, but she got right to business. Not much room for small talk with her. And she was in the business of fundraising. She was good at it. I looked at my notes to collect my thoughts before walking in her office. Instead, she came out the door I was going in.

"Hey, Carl, how are you doing?"

"Great. Thanks. I have just a couple questions for you."

"Well, walk with me. I'm going to the president's office. We'll talk on the way."

She proceeded to march at a vigorous pace. I knew her footsteps very well. She walked faster than anyone in the building.

"What's up?" she asked.

"Well," I said, trying to keep her pace, "just a question about this consultant."

She didn't slow down. She didn't make small talk. I could see how she got stuff done. I explained my dilemma, and she asked, "What do you think Carl?"

"Well, if we go with the first option, it will take longer, and it will cost a bit more. But I wanted to make sure you were OK with that, because Option Two looks cheaper, but I think it will cause some rework."

Having walked at her pace and tracing her thoughts from her questions, I could see that (a) I sounded insecure and uncertain, but (b) my gut told me to stick with option one.

"So yeah, I guess Option A, err. I mean option one." I was trying to sound confident.

"Okay," she said as we arrived at the president's office. "And Carl? In the future don't bring me a question. List the options and bring me your recommendation. Okay?"

"Okay. Yes ma'am," I said as the door shut behind her. "See you later."

She talked with confidence. She walked with confidence, and she dealt with me in a courteous, professional way. I'll bet she didn't spend a lot of time talking about the news or sports or the latest reality show with our janitor.

I started to walk back to my office. And I picked up the pace and walked as is if I had somewhere to go.

Debbie Downer

That night, my brother and Doug had invited me to a meeting.

"Wear a suit," Daniel reminded me on the phone.

"Who's going to be there? Who is this for?" I asked.

"Scott will be there. Do you remember him?"

"Yeah sure." I replied with half-hearted confidence.

"Oh, and Greg, and I think Debbie." All three of them had been at the sales convention.

"Right, Okay," I said. "I'll see you there."

When I walked in, I couldn't believe it. The sales convention had been huge, but it was a nationwide, annual event over a full weekend. This was a monthly meeting and it was just for people in the area.

I saw people who were making way more than I was. I heard people talk about how selling insurance on the side had helped them out financially. I had the same thought I had in Atlanta, "If they can do this, so can I!" I started writing out a monthly schedule for myself. One schedule with the job and one for when I would quit the job. Then I ran the projections and saw that if I kept to my plan I could make six figures.

Chapter Three – Believe!

Even though this was a local meeting, Randy was there. And he talked a lot about having the proper mindset for sales. It was sort of a glass half-full type of discussion, but he really found a way to reach deep inside of me and motivate me.

"It's like the shoe company that sent two sales guys to this island. One guy landed up north on the island, and the other landed on the south part of the island. The first guy called his boss and said, 'Forget it! I'm taking the next flight back. They don't even wear shoes down here!' Then the other sales guy calls his boss and says, 'Boss, you guys better start ramping up production. Everyone here need shoes!'"

He had his own style, and he kept everyone laughing the whole time.

"So, how do YOU look at life?" he asked. "And how are you going to approach life? Do you want to be average?"

The crowd roared back, "NO!"

"Well, do you want to be above average?"

"Yes!"

"What?" he asked in a high-pitched Southern voice. Then he just let a long awkward pause fill the room.

Then he broke the silence, "Do you think average people wanted to be average people? Of course not! They were hoping to be above average. People don't wake up and say, 'I hope to be average someday!' No! The average American was hoping to be above average. And, if we're talking about averages, someone's got to be below average. What do you think they were shooting for? They weren't even trying! So, who ended up being above average? The people shooting for being above average? No! The people who really stand out, the people who really achieve their dreams, the people who dominate their business, they were aiming for excellence."

All the cheering and clapping had stopped, and everyone was

staring at Randy. Well, almost everyone. I couldn't understand what she was saying, but Debbie was grumbling to Doug about something.

"If you want to succeed, you have to set your sights on excellence-perfection- because life is what happens to us when we're making other plans, right?" A couple people laughed. "I see we have some John Lennon fans in here. Okay, so, who said this, 'Everyone has a strategy until they get hit in the face'?"

Someone on the far end of the room shouted.

"That's right! Mike Tyson! The heavyweight champion of the world. Everyone has a strategy until they get hit in the face. So, you have to strive for something beyond what you want. You cannot accept average. And you can't set your sights on above average."

Out of the corner of my eye, I saw Debbie and Doug walking out. Things were far from finished. What were they doing? Were they okay? Did they need help? I decided to follow them out. As I walked over to them, they were having an animated conversation.

Debbie was complaining about what she saw. "Did you see how many people were in there? You know what that means? Fewer leads! Or else Randy's going to give everyone the same leads. I called one of my leads earlier today, and they have already been called twice! Plus the other company is doing web leads. You know what that means, don't you? We'll just get fewer leads and they'll be worse."

Wow. I hadn't thought about any of those things. I looked at Doug and he looked at me.

"Hold on, Debbie," Doug said. "Let me answer Carl, and I'll be right back."

He walked over to me, put his arm around me, and we walked away together.

"Man, don't listen to her," he warned.

Chapter Three – Believe!

"What's her deal anyway?" I asked.

"She's Debbie Downer. You got to stay away from her. You have to surround yourself with people who are going where you want to go."

I felt like a deer in the headlights. Stay away from her? That sounded weird. "What if she's right?" I asked.

"So, what if she is?" he answered.

"How can she not be right? She raised a lot of great questions." I started having doubts.

"But, Carl, if she feels that way, do you think she's going to work those leads hard?"

"No." I rationalized. "Probably not."

"And yes, there were a lot of people in that room. How many of them need to make as much as you do? How many of them are going to work as hard as you? Or how many of them are going to quit or work half-heartedly?"

Doug looked at me with the kind of look that my grandma gave me when she was disappointed in me.

"Carl, people are elevators. When you get in with them, you either go up or you go down. Which way do you want to go?"

"Up," duh.

"Then surround yourself with people who are going where you want to go."

Which one was it? Did I want to believe Debbie? Was I going to land on my feet? Was I a winner? Did my belief determine my income potential? Or was I going back to cubicle land, trying to avoid conversations with Darryl the Janitor?

"Carl, either those people on the island need shoes, or they don't.

But the guy who took the first plane home will never find out, will he? He believed he couldn't, and his beliefs had determined his reality. Henry Ford was one of the greatest inventors of the 20th century, and do you know what he said?"

"What?"

"Whether you believe you can or believe you can't, you're right."

His words hung in the air.

"Me? I decided to believe and look at me! You know how much money I made this week? $6,000."

I tried to do some math. $6,000×2×12.

"Almost $150,000 per year?" I asked.

"What? No!" he said quickly. "Six thousand times 52 weeks is over $300,000!"

I was still thinking in terms of paychecks twice a month. Insurance carriers paid commissions every week.

"Right," I said, shaking my head.

"So – you decide. Either there's no opportunity here, or the opportunity is getting better all the time. I know my income is going up. Just don't listen to her!"

Doors were opening in my mind to rooms I didn't know existed. My intern Isaac had determined his own income, and Debbie was limiting her income potential. All of this was mental. Could Debbie make six figures? Yes, but only if she believed it. So, what about me? Did I believe it? Was I worth that?

Maybe this was all philosophical, but I didn't have time to finish thinking it through. All I had to do was book more appointments and go on them. I put Debbie's thoughts out of my mind and decided to take action.

Chapter Three – Believe!

"Once you start taking action, things will happen," Randy was still talking when I walked back into the conference room.

"Every success I've ever had came from taking action. How about y'all? Has anybody here ever experience success by NOT taking action?"

Silence.

"Anyone?" He paused again. "Has anyone been successful without first taking action?"

No one answered.

"Then BOOM YEAH! Folks, success does not come a-knockin'. Opportunity might, but success don't. You have to go out and turn opportunity into success. Our beliefs are so important. Can you swim across the English Channel?" Randy continued.

The room was silent.

"Someone thought so, and did it. But if you don't think you can, chances are you won't. The English Channel is 150 miles at its widest spot and just under 21 miles at its most narrow spot. Do you think it's possible to swim across it?"

He stopped and took a drink of water.

"But you probably know that someone has crossed it, so naturally you believe it can be done. Dozens of people have done it. Can YOU do it? Not if you think you can't. How fast do you think it can be swum? The first person to do it took nearly 22 hours. Can it be done faster? The world record is 6 hours 55 minutes."

Every so often he stopped and the silence seemed to underscore his message.

"So, do you think it's possible to swim from one side to the other and back again? It's been done. The world record is 16 hours and 10 minutes. Do you think it's possible to swim from one side to the other and then back and then across again? It's been done. The world record is 28 hours and 21 minutes. Whether you think you can or think you can't, you're right. More than anything, life is a mental challenge."

"And, there are channels in YOUR LIFE that can be crossed. There are obstacles to overcome, challenges to conquer. But you won't be able to if you have a limiting belief about yourself. Get rid of your limiting beliefs. Maybe you think, 'I can't earn that much money,' or 'I could never achieve that level of success.' Those are limiting beliefs. Get rid of them!"

"And, here's a question for you," Randy continued. "How much money do you want to make? Someone will say, 'I wanna make a million dollars!' Okay. By when? Because if you just make $50,000 a year, you will eventually make a million dollars. So, what is your annual income goal? How much money do you want to make next year?"

I did the math in my head— $50,000 times 20 years… Let's see, four zeros, five zeros, six zeros. Yep! He's right.

"And when you are out there looking to hire agents, I'm going to let you in on a little secret. It's not really little, it's HUGE." He paused. "This is the way to find out who is going to succeed with sales and who is not going to succeed with sales. Do you want to know how to tell the difference?"

"YES!"

"Do you REALLY want to know how to tell?"

"YES!!" the crowd yelled even louder.

"Okay, I'll tell you. The way to find out whether or not someone is going to be good at sales is to ask them how much they want to make."

His eyes moved across the room making eye contact as they went.

"Ask them. Say, 'How much money do you want to make?' Because they will tell you right then whether they believe in themselves or not. And I'll tell you what, some people don't believe in themselves."

He shrugged his shoulders and imitated a candidate, "Aww, I dunno, $40,000?"

Then he leaned his face toward the crowd and said, "It's like he's asking you a question! 'I dunno, maybe $40,000?' Is he waiting for your approval? Is he trying to figure out how much you'll pay? Is he unsure? Does he not know what his bills are? Does he not have dreams and ambitions?"

As Randy spoke, we were all asking ourselves, "How much money do I want to make?"

"Gang, what's the right answer?" He pretended to ask someone, "How much do you want to make?" Then he pretended to respond, "Who? Me? Well, I, uhhh. I was, ummm."

A few people laughed.

"Go out and buy ya'self some dreams! Because I can't make you want it. And if someone tells you they want to make $40,000, then guess how hard they're going to work? That's right! Until they make $40,000! With us, that would be like the end of April, and I guess they ain't gonna work the rest of the year!"

A few more people laughed.

"It's like we all have this income thermometer deep inside of us. It's set for some amount of money, and when we hit that amount, we just turn off. But until we hit that amount, we'll be like a duck, calm on the surface, but paddlin' like the dickens underneath!"

What he was saying was the logical conclusion of what I had learned about hiring Isaac the intern.

"So, that's my secret for ya. Ask someone how much money they want to make. That will tell you how hard they're willing to work."

There was enough chatter around the room that I could tell people were hearing something they're not used to hearing.

"And here's another secret for ya. If you've got your income thermometer set too low, you know, you can change that."

"BOOM YEAH!"

And right then, somewhere deep inside of me, my income thermometer rose.

What's the Difference?

The next morning as I got ready for work, Randy's words were ringing in my head. How much money did I want to make? But it was more than money. Money is just a way to measure it. I thought about my legacy. What was I going to do to provide for my kids? How was I going to be remembered?

These thoughts were in my head as I drove to work. And that morning I saw something that I think I will never forget.

I turned off a side-street from my neighborhood onto a busier street. I could see seven or eight traffic lights ahead of me. They all turned green at the same time, and my little group of traffic moved forward together. Normally, this road quickly took me through some older parts of town before it landed me four blocks from the parking lot at work. But for some reason we were slowing down.

What's going on? I wondered. We were not on the highway, so I wasn't used to traffic slowing down like this. *Could it be a wreck? Was it just construction?*

We moved forward at a slow but steady pace until I saw red and white lights flashing in circles around a side street. A big fire truck was stopped at an angle blocking all traffic on the side street and disrupting the flow of traffic on the main road. I didn't see any police cars. But I didn't see any smoke either.

Then I saw a group of twenty to thirty men standing in the snow right outside an old building with a sign that read, "The Du-Drop Inn." It was a bar. There were twenty to thirty disheveled, tired, middle-aged men standing outside a bar where apparently a fire alarm had gone off.

Most of the men were smoking cigarettes. One of them was chewing tobacco, and leaned over into the street to spit. A couple of young firefighters scurried in and out of the building. It looked like no one was hurt. There weren't any fire hoses setup. An ambulance had just pulled away, without its lights and sirens on. There were no casualties.

Then it hit me. It was 8:10 in the morning! What were these guys doing at a bar at 8:10 in the morning?

"They had probably worked the graveyard shift," Amy said later when I told her about it. She always saw the best in people.

"Okay, but at 8 in the morning? On a weekday? I'd be getting some rest. Or getting my kids to school. But to be at a bar at 8 in the morning in the middle of the week?" I was dumbfounded.

"They probably can't get a good job," my friend Joe rationalized when I told him about it. "If I couldn't get a good job, I might end up in a place like that."

"But at 8AM on a weekday?" I asked. "You wouldn't do that," I countered.

"Maybe not," he said. Joe was one of the most strait-laced guys I knew. "But what's the difference between us and them?"

But I just couldn't get that out of my mind. As I put my thoughts together, it occurred to me that those men chose to be where they were. They didn't believe they could achieve anything more.

For me, it hit close to home. My Dad was an alcoholic. He left my family when I was seven. The few times that I saw him, he would finish at least one pack of cigarettes for breakfast, and he could make a 12-pack of beer disappear on an average weeknight. Eventually, my Dad would die alone while living in a hotel in a third-world country. The staff at the hotel didn't discover his body until he had been dead for a couple days.

Joe's question kept ringing in my head, "What's the difference between us and them?"

Now, I'm not here to belittle my father. I'm also not a psychologist who's trying to analyze the social, economic and educational circumstances of one person over another. But I've come to the conclusion that one thing can make a difference: belief.

Nobody dreams about dying alone in a third-world country while living in a cheap hotel with no property to his name. Nobody has dreams of being mediocre. I think the difference is belief. Do you believe you deserve better than that? Do you believe you're capable of more than that? Or are you willing to settle for second-rate? There is a hunger in the human heart for more. But that hunger can die out. Or rather, that hunger can be killed. By what? By our thoughts. By our belief.

If we believe we don't deserve good things in exchange for delivering value, then we probably won't get good things. If we don't believe we're capable of greatness, our minds probably won't search out all possibilities until a path to greatness is achieved. If we agree to settle for less, then that's what we'll get.

My story is not a get-rich-quick scheme. What I'm really talking about is prosperity and fulfillment as opposed to fortune and fame. And I'm not measuring anybody in financial terms here. It just so happens that for me, as a provider for my family, I need to make more money. I choose to believe that I can accomplish more because I must find a way to provide for my growing family. I can because I must. Failure is not an option.

Now maybe you want to stop at a bar for a burger and a beer on a Wednesday night. Heck, you might want to stop after a late shift. I'm not going to judge you. But if you don't believe that you are capable of greatness, if you don't believe you have been given talents to make a difference, if you don't believe that there must be a way to achieve your goals and your dreams, then you are burying your treasure in a field for fear of failure.

The human heart has conceived of and achieved a passage from earth to the moon. We can capture the image of a memory on a hand-held device and within moments send that to a satellite in space and have it routed to the person of our choosing five hundred miles away within a split second. We can identify what is happening in a human body at the cellular level and prescribe medications or procedures that will stop diseases. These things are only possible because someone first believed they were possible!

The power of belief is fast enough to send messages at the speed of light, bright enough to light up the night sky on the 4th of July. The power of belief is strong enough to move mountains— even if it's only one truckload at a time.

What limit is there to what can be accomplished when we believe?

Rear View Mirror — What We Learned in Chapter Three

- The way we look at the world determines everything. We must believe in ourselves or else no one else will.
- If we want to succeed, we must aim for excellence.
- We must surround ourselves with people who are going where we want to go.
- Success only comes from taking action.
- We all have income thermometers. They tell us what we think we're worth. We are not likely to make more than what our income thermometer is set at, but we CAN change our income thermometers.
- If we agree to settle for less, then that's probably what we'll get.

Chapter Three Exercises

1. Write your goal down here again.

   (If you haven't written down a goal, realize that you are less likely to achieve your goal than if you just took the time to write it down.)

   If it has changed since Chapter 1, how has it changed?

My Goals:

_____

_____

2. What limiting beliefs do you have that prevent you from achieving your goals?

_____

_____

3. In your work relationships, are you more like Darryl, or more like Terri? How can you become more like Terri?

_____

_____

4. Who in your life is a Debbie Downer? How can you protect your dreams from that person?

_____

_____

5. How much money do you want to make?
   (i.e., what is your income thermometer set at?)

_____

_____

_____

6. What do you believe you can achieve? If you haven't
   written down goals, then write some down now!

_____

_____

_____

7. What actions can you take *TODAY* that will best help you
   meet your goals?

_____

_____

8. What actions can you take *EVERY DAY* that will best
   help you meet your goals?

_____

_____

4. REVERSE.
(TURN THINGS AROUND)

Road Map — What We'll Learn in This Chapter
- People make decisions based on emotion and they justify them logically.
- People may forget what you said — but they will never forget how you made them feel.
- Why you should never say, "Thanks for your business" and what you should say instead.
- It's easier to achieve a goal that you first visualize.

Why Am I Here?

My hands were sweaty as I knocked on the door. A man with a blue, short-sleeved shirt met me at the door. He wiped his hands on a rag and held out his hand. Above his chest pocket was an embroidered white tag with the name, Matt in a handwritten font.

"I'm..."

"Matt," we said together.

"C'mon in," he finished and he swung the door closed behind me and turned around.

He and his wife, Susie, lived in a modest tri-level. A dinosaur, a toy tractor, and a light saber were strewn on the ground in front of the T.V.

"Bob the Builder, can we fix it?" chimed the characters on the screen. The T.V. was on, but no one was in the living room. "Yes, we can!"

I walked past a glass cabinet with dozens of miniature figurines of all shapes. They were all obviously made by the same company, but I couldn't have guessed the name of the collection. Matt led me to the kitchen table. That's very important. If our prospects won't meet in the kitchen, they don't mean business.

"This is my wife, Susie," Matt introduced us.

"Nice to meet you. Just gimme a sec," she said as she wiped the table and removed a small pile of plates to the sink.

After we sat down, I looked at them one by one.

"Matt, Susie," I said slowly, "Is this the letter you sent in to us?"

"Yep. That's it," Matt said, matter-of-factly.

"OK. Well, I assume the reason you sent this in is that you both want to make sure that you're okay if anything happens to you. Matt, is that right?"

"That'd be nice."

It wasn't a great response, but I really wanted to close this deal, and

I didn't want to push back in any way that would cause me to lose it. Amy sure didn't need me coming home empty-handed. Not that she ever put any pressure on me. I did plenty of that myself, but I wanted to be successful for her as much as for myself. So I explained the benefits of mortgage protection.

"Some people think the mortgage protection only covers the amount you owe on your house. That's not true. The level of protection stays the same throughout the life of your mortgage."

I went on to explain a little more about the product. Then I told him the price, and I started filling out the application.

"Have you ever had a heart attack, stroke, TIA, or cancer?"

I probably said some of the questions wrong. I don't remember skipping any questions, but it's possible. I really wanted to make this work, and I didn't want to lose the sale.

"Have you ever had suicidal thoughts? Any plans to go skydiving in the next two years?"

I went through the questionnaire, and the anticipation of their reaction grew. Would it be an easy sale or was I wasting my time?

"OK, I need you to sign here, and I need one check for $75 and one for $84."

"Whoa! Hold on. We didn't say we were going through with this."

I must've thought I could slip that in without anyone noticing. I should've realized that I had not done enough to build rapport or gain their trust.

"But, I thought you wanted to get coverage in place." What a lame excuse!

The logical part of me wanted to say, "Hey man! What were you thinking? You just gave me your birth date, Social Security number, driver's license number, and your medical history. What did you think would happen?"

But that is the point. He wasn't thinking logically. He was thinking emotionally. After all, that's how we all make decisions. We make decisions based on emotions, and we justify them logically. If I put it another way, I would say, we make decisions based on trust, and then we justify them based on value.

How we think and how we feel are very important. But feelings are the first level of defense. No one will do business with you if they don't trust, and feel good about you, the product, service, the sale, or whatever.

I learned a very valuable lesson that day. I didn't want to EVER go through the process of qualifying a prospect, setting an appointment, driving to meet them, and spending time with them only to fumble the close.

Amy Helps

"How did tonight go?" she asked as I put my briefcase down.

I could have just said, "Fine." But I didn't. I swallowed my pride and decided to tell her. And I am glad I did because that's how I learned how valuable her feedback is.

"Not good," I said. "I blew it." I fell backwards onto the couch.

"What do you mean?" she asked, sitting with her hands on her knees and leaning in to our conversation.

"I blew it. I could have closed it, but instead, I blew it. I didn't build enough rapport."

"What happened?" She wanted details.

"I sat down with them and asked if they sent in the letter we got. The guy said, 'Yes,' so, I asked if it was important for them to get the coverage in place in order to protect each other, in case something happened to the other one. He replied with a casual, 'That'd be nice.'"

"Doesn't sound very genuine to me," Amy observed. "What did

you do next?"

"I explained the coverage and started filling out the application." I said.

"OK, you have to tell them before you fill out the application that they're going to write you a check. It should probably go something like this: 'OK, here's all I can do for you, because I can't approve this policy. But what I can do is submit your application with your deposit for the first month's' payment, and I can see if we can get you approved. Does that make sense?'"

It made a lot of sense to me.

"You're on their side," she added. "You're helping them."

That didn't just make sense, it was brilliant. As a matter fact, it's almost exactly what I had already been taught. I skipped that part of the script that night because I didn't want them to say, "No" to me that early in my presentation.

Why is this step so important? Amy explained. "One thing I learned from teaching is a quote from Carl Buehner. I don't know who he is, but I remember his name because I heard this when we started dating. He said, 'They may forget what you said — but they will never forget how you made them feel.'"

REVERSE

Randy said it well when he quoted Teddy Roosevelt, "People don't care how much you know until they know how much you care."

What this means is that you can't make a sale if it's all about **you**.

The "P" in "PRNDL" stands for "*PARK*." And the point is that you can't move someone out of park.

The second point is "R" and it stands for "*REVERSE*."

This second point deals with the reason to buy. People buy for their own reasons, not for your reasons. They don't care about your interests. While they don't want to be forced to buy, they expect a sales person to be pushy. They expect a sales person is interested in nothing but themselves. We have to **REVERSE** that. We have to make it all about **them**.

Randy made this point very clear. "People are only tuned in to one radio station: WiiFM. That stands for, 'What's in it for me?' People expect greasy salespeople to push them. You do not want to be lumped in with all other sales people. You want to **REVERSE** things. When you do, it changes everything. When you turn things around, it throws them off their game of holding you at arm's length."

This resonated so strongly with me.

"People like to buy, but people don't like to be sold."

Reversing things just means showing the prospect that you care about their needs more than you care about your needs.

Fortunately, there are many ways to put things in "Reverse." You can either give your prospect a gift, a compliment, or something to show them that their satisfaction is more important than your sale. When you **REVERSE** things and show your prospect that you care about them, you demonstrate trust. You make them feel special. You show them what's in it for them.

This brings us to one of my least favorite expressions: "Thanks for your business!" When you say that, you're telling your client that you are profiting from this exchange. Why would you want to leave them with that thought? That puts them in a place to take their business elsewhere.

Amy and I were refinancing our mortgage one time when I grew suspicious of the loan officer. She told us that we had the best deal possible. When we told her someone else made us a better offer, she changed the terms and countered with the same terms we found somewhere else. Out of loyalty, Amy said she would not switch. The loan officer replied in an email by saying, "Thanks for your business." At that point it was obvious that she wasn't helping us. She was helping herself. We switched to the better offer.

Later on, when I enhanced my script, I'd ask my clients, "Have I done a good job for you here today?" Or I would ask, "Was I able to help you find the coverage you need?" These questions better represent the reality that I am a professional who is on their side. It was a lot better than saying, "Well, thanks to you, now I'm going to be able to go to a nice steakhouse with my wife." And one of the things I make sure all my clients do is get rid of the "thanks for your business" message. Instead, I encourage them to write, "Thanks for trusting me/us with your business." This puts the focus on an exchange of *trust*, not just *money*.

This is also one of the reasons I hate the word "actually." When I hear that word, I know someone is trying to convince me— maybe against my will. The word "actually" has a connotation that the audience is stupid and needs to be set right. It creates a tone of superiority. "Actually, I'm right and you should listen to me." If you use this word, you may find yourself subtly thinking less of your prospects. Instead, we need to be motivated to help our prospects. Avoid the word "actually."

Visualization

The next day, I told Doug about what I had learned.

"Yep. You should have listened to Randy," he said, in a friendly but disciplinary way.

"I know."

"But hey, you learned something. You learned the value of showing them you care. You probably won't forget that part of the script from now on, will you?" To ask the question was to answer it. "Hey, let's get together for lunch, okay? My treat."

"Sounds good," I wasn't about to turn down a free lunch.

"Where do you want to eat?" he asked.

"I don't know. How about Steak-n-Shake?" I asked.

"Nah, how about Olive Garden? We'll celebrate!" he said.

Chapter Four – Reverse!

"Celebrate what?" I asked.

"You learning the importance of showing them you care!"

I was surprised that he would take the time to meet me for lunch, as though he didn't have better things to do.

We pulled into the parking lot at the same time, and we were soon ordering our food.

"It's crazy how delicate each sale can be," I said to Doug, as I handed the menu to our waiter. "I mean, one little thing here or one little thing there, and bam! The sale is lost."

"That's why you have to follow the script," Doug said. "It's battle-tested. It works."

"I am just surprised at how much emotion plays into the decision," I said, matter-of-factly.

"You're too logical. People aren't logical. They make decisions based on feelings."

"But this is insurance," I objected. "It's pretty straightforward. Isn't it?"

"No way! It's all about emotion," Doug countered.

"But there's the amount of coverage. There's the premiums, and the amount of coverage is based on the mortgage. Either it makes sense, or it doesn't." I was confused.

"No, it's more about, 'Do you feel like you got a good deal?' Or, 'Do you feel like this will take care of your kids if you die?' Or, 'Do you feel like a responsible adult if you get this coverage?' It's all about emotions."

I was trying to make sense of it.

"By the look on your face, I can tell that this doesn't feel right to you, does it?" He asked with a broad grin on his face.

"No. It doesn't. Why wouldn't people make decisions logically?" I was missing his point completely.

"But listen to yourself, it doesn't feel right to you, but logically, you've seen it happen? Feelings play a big part of it." Doug could tell I wasn't convinced, despite the irony that my observations didn't feel right.

So he went on. "I was just reading about a plastic surgeon who found that some of his patients didn't like the way they looked after literally getting a new face that they had chosen! They still felt bad about themselves. So, he started working with them to change the way they viewed things before the surgery. He realized he didn't need to change the way they looked to others, but he needed to change the way they looked to themselves. This led to visualization techniques used by lots of athletes today."

"That's crazy! Get plastic surgery and still hate the way you look?"

"Exactly, because it's all about feelings. And here's the thing-because of this guy's research, he went on to test to see if the brain can tell the difference between actual experiences and experiences that are imagined. And it can't! If the brain imagines experiences with enough intensity of emotions, it cannot tell the difference between real or imagined experiences."

"That's crazy," I sneered.

"But world-class athletes use this. They visualize success. Edwin C. Moses did it with running the hurdles. Andre Agassi did it with playing tennis. They imagined perfect execution in their heads so much that eventually it was as if they had practiced with perfect execution. It's easier to achieve a goal that you first visualize."

"What are you saying? That I should visualize meeting with prospects?" I asked.

"It might not hurt. But what I'm saying is that if your brain is the source of all logic and it can't tell the difference between actual memories and imagined memories that were connected to strong emotions, then why can't you see that feelings trump logic?"

Chapter Four – Reverse!

He had a good point.

"And people don't care how much you know…"

We finished the sentence together, "Until they know how much you care!"

After lunch, I was thinking about everything Doug said. I realized that Doug was practicing what he preached. He took me to lunch. He talked with me. He listened to me complain.

He was helping me get started because it helped him as an agency manager, but I started to accept and believe what he was teaching me because I knew how much he cared. He was willing to go out of his way to help me.

Had he offered the same teaching content in a different way, I might have blown him off, but here I was, grateful that he took me out to lunch. I realized that he could help me because he was making a personal investment in me.

This is what I needed to convey to my prospects. I needed to show them that even though I was the professional, I wanted what was best for them.

If I approached my prospects as though they were interrupting me or as though I didn't have time for people who didn't want to buy from me, I wouldn't have many clients.

People don't care how much you know until they know how much you care.

People will never forget the way you make them feel.

And "turning things around" during the sale is one of the best ways to demonstrate that.

I looked back at this section of the script:
-Now, I can't get you approved for this coverage.
-What I can do is explain how this coverage works. Then we can submit an application with the first month's premium to see if we

can get it approved.

-Does that make sense?

This part of the script was turning things around. I could have said, "Let's get this application going as soon as we can."

I could have made it look like it was up to me to get the coverage in place.

I could have been pushy and overbearing and asked our prospects to help me win a vacation from a sales conference.

But I agreed to set aside what I thought in favor of the battle-tested approach.

Rear View Mirror — What We Learned in Chapter Four

- People make decisions based on emotion and they justify them logically.
- People may forget what we say — but they will never forget how we made them feel.
- By putting things in **REVERSE**, we can show our prospects that we care more about them than we do about making the sale.
- See the Appendix for examples of using the second part of The PRNDL Process: **REVERSE.**
- Why we should never say, "Thanks for your business." Instead, we should say, "Thanks for **trusting** me/us with your business."
- Avoid using the word "actually" in your dialogue with clients and prospects.
- It's easier to achieve a goal that we first visualize.

Chapter Four Exercises

1. Thinking about your product/ service/ solution, list 3 **logical** reasons someone should trust you with their business.

1.)
_____

2.)
_____

3.)
_____

2. Thinking about your product/ service/ solution, list 3 **emotional** reasons someone should trust you with their business.

1.)
_____

2.)
_____

3.)
_____

3. Which of these two sets of reasons do you focus on in your script/messaging? List examples of how you can leverage the emotional reasons more.

_____

_____

_____

_____

4. Thinking back to previous sales you've closed, list some examples of how you've demonstrated that you care about the prospect more than the sale.

_____

_____

_____

_____

5. From observation of previous sales, what can you do for or say to other prospects in the future to demonstrate your willingness to put them first?

_____

_____

_____

_____

6. Do you use a phrase like, "actually" or "to be honest," or "as a matter of fact"? If so, stop saying it.
7. Do you use the phrase, "Thanks for your business"? If so, make a resolution to change it now. Instead, say, "Thanks for trusting me/us with your business."

Chapter Four – Reverse!

5. YOUR DESTINATION

Road Map — What We'll Learn in This Chapter
- The importance of writing your goals down.
- The difference between "toward" goals and "away" goals.
- The reason goals need to reflect the present, not the future.
- The importance of having a daily/weekly performance goal and a monthly/quarterly outcome goal.

Setting Goals

By now, I was almost in the top 100 on the leaderboard. I was close to leaving the job I was in and going out on my own. I had learned so much.

- Winners land on their feet.
- Trading time for money can be a trap.
- Fish don't complain about being wet.
- We determine our own income levels.
- You must have RFW's to succeed.
- We must take responsibility for the circumstances we choose.

Reviewing the Steps

Sales was becoming less mysterious. By following the script, I was able to control the sale. When I got off the script, I crashed. Every encounter with a prospect would begin by highlighting the fact that we were not in "*PARK.*" I reminded the prospect of the steps they had already taken. Not only was I keeping things focused on them, but I was reminding myself where they were and where I needed to lead them next.

Putting the sale in "*REVERSE*" helped me to keep in mind that I was serving the client. And it also helped show the client that I cared. This interaction was about them and not about me. I was there for them. They weren't there for me.

This has nothing to do with "Reverse Psychology." **REVERSE** simply means that we have to have a mindset that we are in sales, not to make more money or pursue our own interests. We have to genuinely be motivated by helping our clients. By putting our client first, we are turning things around. The stereotype of a sales person is that they are pushing for the sale. We have to turn that idea completely around. We have to turn the tables on that idea.

But I still had a lot to learn about sales. So I went to another sales meeting, in the hopes of learning more.

Aim at Nothing and you WILL hit it!

I sat next to Greg and we talked after a sales meeting. "How long have you been doing this?" I asked.

"This is my third year," he replied as we got our free refills at a late-night fast food restaurant.

"Wow- third year?" I asked.

"Well, this will be my third year, but it's only really my second *full* year."

"What do you mean?" I asked.

"Well," he sighed, "I've been to two year-end conferences, but only one of them was for a full year's work."

"Okay," I said, not knowing why he was making the distinction.

"The year-end conference is awesome," he said enthusiastically.

"Is it like the one we went to in Atlanta?"

"No way. It's much bigger!"

"Really? How?"

"The year-end conference is where everyone gets their income rings. It's a huge celebration. It's so exciting."

"Cool," I said. "When did you get your first income ring?"

"Aww, man, I don't have one yet." His excitement turned to remorse. "They only have income rings for $100,000 and $200,000 and on and on. I made less than $100,000, so I didn't get one." I didn't want to insult him, but I couldn't understand it. How could these other people be doing so well and Greg not be doing so well?

"Are you going to get one this year?" I asked, trying to be tactful.

"I hope so. I think so. I want to."

"Well, you've been doing great. You're always on the leaderboard. What's your goal for this year?" I asked.

"I don't really have a goal for this year." He hesitated. "Well, I guess I want to get an income ring." He seemed so unsure of himself. "And, yeah, I have a good month and then I fizzle out. Then I have a good month and then I have a bad month. You've just been seeing my good month. I'm my own worst enemy."

"Well," I said, trying to be encouraging, "what's your work plan?"

"What do you mean?" he asked.

"I mean, how many days do you plan to be out in the field running appointments?"

"Well," he said, "some days are better than others. I don't know. I just get out there and sell. Anyway, it's getting late and I gotta get home."

I was glad that he gave a reason to end that discussion. I couldn't understand him. I started thinking about my work plan.

In order for me to be able to leave my job, I would have to hit a specific amount of additional income. By now, I had also identified the math behind the sales and I could predict my income.

If I made 100 phone calls, I would book three appointments.
If I booked 3 appointments, I would submit two applications.
For every 10 applications I submitted, seven would get approved.
My average annual premium was $94.
Starting out, that meant I would earn $620 in commissions.
So, if I called to book appointments three days a week, I would book 9 appointments, submit 6 applications, get 4 approved and earn $2,480.

"Carl, do you know your numbers?" Doug began helping me define my goals on the phone the next day.

"I think so," I replied cautiously.

"Okay. So, how much money do you want to make? Let's start there and work our way back."

"Well, I'd like to make at least $100,000."

"At least?"

"Yeah, at least. I mean it would be nice to make more, but…"

"But what?" he interrupted.

"But, first things first," I said, trying to sound confident.

"Let me ask you this, Carl. Do you think people are more

motivated to earn money or more motivated to protect against losing money they've already earned?"

"Well," I stopped. "I don't know, but I don't have money. I mean, if I was already making $100,000, that would be a different story."

"Okay, he reframed the question. "Let's talk about weight loss, then."

"Weight loss? What are you talking about? I thought we're talking about income goals."

"We are," he continued. "And we're building a plan for you to hit your goals. So, let's make sure to set a plan to motivate you. Do you realize how much we Americans spend on unhealthy food? And how much we spend trying to lose the weight we put on? When we Americans set a goal of living healthy, we are typically setting a goal to lose weight. And we are professionals when it comes to losing weight. Try this diet and that diet and we keep losing the same 20 pounds. Why does it not work? Why, when we set weight-loss goals, do we gain the weight back?"

"Because we're lazy?" I asked.

"Maybe. Yes. But I think it's because we set goals in the wrong way."

"Right. We should use S.M.A.R.T. goals, right?" I asked jokingly. Every manager at the university had been taught to make S.M.A.R.T. goals. Specific, measurable, attainable, relevant, time-bound goals.

"Forget that for a minute. There are two main motivators for all human choices. Two main things that drive human decisions. What are they?"

I knew he was looking for something specific, but I didn't want to guess wrong, "I don't know."

"OK, why do you want to make some money?" he asked.

"To provide for my family."

"OK, so, you want something. It could be financial stability, vacation, prestige, whatever. Right?"

"Okay," I said, trying to guess where he was going next.

"What might be some of the different reasons people want to make money?" he asked.

"I thought you said there were only two motivators."

"Right. Okay—so, let's go back to a goal of living healthy. What could be a motivator there?"

"Lose weight?" I asked.

"Exactly! Losing weight is a motivation, but it's a different type of motivation from wanting to go on a vacation, or build a dream house, or provide for your family. You see?" he asked. "All motivation is either toward something or away from something. Does that make sense?"

"Yes, but how does this relate to setting an income goal?"

"It matters how you frame your goal. When it comes to weight loss or living healthy — which is a better goal? Towards good health or away from a specific weight?"

I thought about it and finally said, "I don't know."

"In the short-term, we are more motivated to protect against loss. People will work much harder to prevent a loss of $100,000 than they will to earn $100,000. But that only works in the short term."

This was starting to make sense. He continued, "If someone sees 250 pounds on the scale, they may think to themselves, 'Whoa! I've gained too much! I need to lose weight.' So, they set out to lose weight. What happens when they hit 240? The thing that motivated them is less motivating. They rationalize with themselves saying, '250 is bad, but 240 isn't THAT bad.' So they scale back on their weight loss effort. They cheat here and there. Pretty soon, they're right back where they started."

"So, how do I translate that into my income goals?" I asked.

"OK, well you said you wanted to make 'at least' $100K. That sounds a little weak as a goal. Once you hit $100,000, will you stop? Or what if you make $90,000? Will you think that was good enough? Your goal sounds more like you're trying to get out of debt. Why not set a more ambitious goal, like, I want to put my kids through college and build a lake house for the summer?"

"Well, that would be nice," I thought.

"Just like losing weight would be nice? Instead you want to set a goal of living healthy – eating right and staying active. You've got to make your goal a positive goal. The goal of where you are going, rather than what you are avoiding."

"Okay, I think I see the difference," I said.

"Another thing, Carl, your long-term goal has to be fueled by moving towards a goal instead of moving away. And you need to say *when* you plan to achieve your goal."

"So– like, I want to make enough money to pay for college in eight years and buy a lake house in, let's say three years?"

"Wrong," said Doug, with a smile that betrayed his correction.

"Let's go back to weight loss. If a 250-pound guy says, "I want to lose 50 pounds by Christmas," then all his energy is in the future. He'll never lose the 50 pounds, because his focus is on what will happen in the future. His focus needs to be on today."

Doug stopped. He was making a lot of sense. It was like I could see the picture of the puzzle on the box, but when I looked at the disassembled pieces, I was overwhelmed.

"You know, Carl, my business turned around when I looked at my goals in the right way. A friend called me one day and asked how my business was going and I said, 'My goal is to be profitable next year.' He called me the next year and I still hadn't hit my goal, but I still had the goal. When he called the third year in a row and we had the same conversation for a third time, that's when my goal changed. My goal became, 'I want to grow my net revenue this and every month by 5%.' Once I did that, it forced me to make better decisions every day. And I became profitable that month, and my revenue has grown 5% or more every month."

"I think annual goals are too far away. The closer they are to the present, the more control you have. I recommend having a monthly outcome goal and a daily performance goal. And you can shift to a quarterly outcome goal and a weekly performance goal. But make sure the focus is on the present and remember 'towards' goals are more effective in the long run than 'away' goals are."

"Wow- this is stressful," I complained.

"Carl, stress comes from having the same unresolved thought more than once. What you need is a system you can trust so that you don't need to have the same unwanted thought more than once. Write your goals down. Have a short-term performance goal and a monthly outcome goal or target. Then, instead of worrying about it and having the same stressful thought over and over, look at your goals every day. Read them out loud. Get excited about them."

I still had some stress. "What if...?" I started.

"And, Carl, you will come across 'what ifs.' You will come across obstacles. You will hit road blocks. But you can't control those things. Control the things you can control and put your focus there. Don't focus on things you can't control."

I thought about Greg and how he didn't have a plan, so he didn't get the results he wanted.

I decided to let the stress go. I made goals and I kept my focus there.

My daily performance goal became, "Make 100 calls a day, three days a week."

My monthly outcome goal became, "$25,000 of annual business each month."

Rear View Mirror — What We Learned in Chapter Five
- Goals should be written down. Goals that are not written are just dreams.
- There are two main motivators for all human choices- *towards* pleasure/opportunity/gain and *away* from pain/risk/loss.
- "Toward" goals are better than "away" goals.
- Goals need to reflect the present, not the future.
- Make a daily/weekly performance goal and a monthly/quarterly outcome goal.
- Stress comes from having the same unresolved thought more than once. We need a system we can trust so that we don't need to have the same unwanted thought more than once

Chapter Five Exercises
1. Write your goal down from the previous chapter. Write several goals if necessary.

_____

_____

_____

_____

_____

_____

2. How can you write your goals so that they are "towards" goals instead of "away" goals?

_____

_____

_____

_____

_____

_____

3. How can you write your goals so that they are focused on the present? (today, this week, this month, this quarter)

_____

_____

_____

_____

_____

4. How can you write your goals so that you have 1 or 2 outcomes and 1 or 2 performance goals?

_____

_____

_____

6. FINDING NEUTRAL

Road Map — What We'll Learn in This Chapter
- The importance of presenting yourself as the indifferent professional.
- The value of citing a third-party that is recognized, verified, authorized, endorsed, or certified.

Tom Brady the Cat

The few spots of clouds made the denim blue sky seem higher than ever. Two vapor trails drew my eyes from one horizon to the other.

Saturdays like this made me wish I were cooking on the grill at home with my kids. It's hard to enjoy a beautiful day from behind a sun visor or from a cubicle.

Reluctantly, I pulled into the driveway of my afternoon appointment. I gave myself a short pep talk, encouraging me to keep focused on my work.

Chapter Six – Finding Neutral

Tom met me at the door. He was a single dad and seemed like a good guy.

"Brady, get off the table," he shoved his cat with his arm until the cat landed on the ground. Apparently, he was a New England Patriots fan.

"I named him after Tom Brady," he informed me with a smile.

"Oh, okay." I answered, pretending that I hadn't already figured that out.

"Now, who are you with?" he asked.

"I'm with the Mortgage Protection Center," I said, which was just a generic name that told people what we did.

His kitchen table had worn well over the years. He brushed some crumbs off the table with his forearm for me to get my laptop out. His kitchen was not any messier than anyone else's kitchen. But it was clearly the kitchen of a home without a woman's touch.

"You don't work for Milford Savings and Loan?" he asked.

"No sir," I said as I plugged my laptop in and got my papers together.

He turned over a copy of the letter he had sent us. The letter was paper-clipped to the envelope it came in. "It says Milford Savings and Loan here," pointing to the return address on the envelope.

"That's right." I tried to ignore what he was implying. "Your mortgage is through Milford Savings and Loan for…" I ran my finger across my copy of his letter. "$150,000. Is that right?"

"Yes. But how did you get this information?" his apprehension was turning to skepticism.

I wanted to say, "You sent that into us." Or I could have said, "Sir, that's public information available at the courthouse." But evidently I hesitated just a moment too long.

"Can I see your driver's license?" he asked.

"Sure," I called his bluff, or whatever it was.

The tables were turned. Normally I should ask him for his driver's license. After all, I suppose someone could be trying to scam him out of a check for $83. And I suppose anyone can try to commit insurance fraud, too. I'm just not smart enough to scam anyone one way or the other. And I sure wouldn't risk a jail sentence to make another sale or two. But if I were planning to scam him, I would probably have a fake I.D.

"Milford Savings and Loan doesn't specialize in mortgage protection. That's where we come in. We do the mortgage protection for a lot of their clients." I provided the shortest pause possible before pivoting back and trying to recover lost ground.

From memory, I wanted to say, "Is this the letter you sent us?" But the question really didn't apply anymore. And his wife was not there, so I couldn't go to the next step without changing it all around.

"Everyone has different reasons for protecting their mortgage. But is that your daughter outside?" I interrupted myself.

"Yes." His answer was empty. He was reading my driver's license as though it were a mystery novel.

"I assume you want to make sure she's taken care of in case anything should happen to you. Is that right?"

"Yes, but why didn't this come from Milford Savings and Loan? They are the ones I got the mortgage through. This letter doesn't even say Mortgage Protection Center. Are you guys endorsed by Milford?" He put my driver's license down and took off his glasses.

This made me very uncomfortable. I wasn't doing anything wrong, so I didn't like the fact that he had my driver's license. The sale was going nowhere and I didn't want to be rude or make a scene.

"We work with homeowners like yourself around the country with all kinds of lenders."

I knew that if I sounded defensive, he would take that as confirmation that I was trying to scam him. So I kept calm.

"I don't work out the relationships with different vendors. My job is just to help people plan for coverage to see if we can get that approved." I was working on step number two: turn things around.

"Did you want to apply to see if you can get approved?" I continued.

"I don't know," he said as he looked at the letter we sent him.

Now it seemed that any time spent here was going to be wasted. The sale was mine to lose.

"You can't lose what you don't have," I remembered Randy saying on a conference call. And I didn't have this sale yet.

So I stood up and put my jacket on and grabbed my laptop bag.

"I understand completely. Can I have my driver's license back since you won't be needing it?"

He looked alarmed at my response and interrupted me by saying, "No, no, no, it's OK. I'm sorry. Please sit down."

"Is it important for you to see if we can get this coverage in place?" I asked. Now I was the one who was skeptical.

"Yes."

"Okay," I said as I took my jacket off, sat down, and took my driver's license back.

"You don't know your driver's license number, do you?" I asked as I started filling out his application.

Before long, I got his check and application and put them in my briefcase. He was now a client.

The Conference Call

I got in my car and set my GPS with the address to my next appointment. Since it was a Saturday, there were no conference calls to dial into. But I did have a recorded training call that I could listen to as I drove to my next appointment.

"You are the professional," Randy said on the recorded training call. "You are making a recommendation to your client. You don't need to prove anything. You should act like the professional."

He continued, "When you go to the doctor's office, what does he do, ask if you would consider taking your pants off? No! He tells you to take your pants off and fold them over the chair. And you do it. Why? Because he's the professional."

"You need to be an indifferent professional, like that doctor is. It's the same attitude you should have with your clients. You need to direct them to the kitchen table. You need to ask them for their driver's license. You need to ask them for their Social Security number. Don't wring your hands about small things like that. Take charge. Tell them what to. You are the professional and the prospect wants to be advised and directed by someone who knows what they're doing."

Yep. When Tom Brady's owner asked me for my driver's license, he took control of the appointment. I was able to take control back, but that sale could have fallen apart just as easily.

There were two things going on here. First, as the sales person, I needed to portray a professional— an authority. We tend to trust the accredited, licensed, impartial professional more than we trust the run of the mill salesperson. Why? For the same reason "putting things in **REVERSE**" is so important. Because an impartial person isn't trying to "sell us." Because when someone is an indifferent professional as opposed to someone with a conflict of interest, it is less likely that they will profit from our choices. And no one likes to feel like they got the bad end of a deal.

Secondly, and maybe more importantly, Tom was looking for the authority that came from his bank. He trusted his bank already, obviously, or he wouldn't have financed his mortgage through them.

Did we work with his bank's clients? Yes. Did we work for the bank? No.

We were borrowing authority from his bank by listing the name of his bank with his mortgage amount. Looking back, I'm sure other clients made the assumption that we were from their bank, even though we weren't.

What I learned from this was the power that a **NEUTRAL**, third-party has in influencing a purchasing decision. And this is magnified when the third party is verified, authorized, endorsed, or certified by another established, trustworthy institution.

Explaining *NEUTRAL*

This became the next part of the PRNDL process. In Step One, we get prospects out of *"PARK"* by reminding them of everything they've already done in the journey towards becoming our client. In Step Two, we *"REVERSE"* things. We do something for our prospects and show them that we are there to serve them.

The third step is *"NEUTRAL."*

The *"NEUTRAL"* step is best played after *"PARK"* and *"REVERSE,"* but it might come up at other times. Very simply, the step involves drawing on a third-party authority, a neutral party. This is not to be confused with a competitor or other prospects or clients. The step should focus on someone who has no vested interest in whether your prospect becomes a client. And this neutral third-party should not, in anyway, profit from your sales.

The classic neutral third-party commercial is "4 out of 5 dentists recommend..." The buyer is won over because these dentists have nothing to gain by promoting this product. And who is the buyer to question authority?

Regardless of whether the prospect buys, and regardless of who they buy from – the authority should be undisputed. The authority could be government studies, market research, the Census Bureau, or other sources.

Other Examples

Looking back on mortgage protection, there weren't a lot of ways to capitalize on *"NEUTRAL"* because the implied connection to the Mortgage Protection Center served that need.

Later on, as a sales and marketing consultant, I found lots more opportunities to use this third step of appealing to a neutral authority.

Al, for example was the plant manager for a specialized manufacturing company and I met with him twice a month to plan and execute communications with prospects and clients. He would describe the situation and tell me what he wanted to say and I would look for ways to enhance his message. Naturally, I used the PRNDL process.

While reviewing his prospects, Al came to one and said, "This one's easy. He called me yesterday while I was out, so I just need to tell him, 'I was out of the office yesterday. Here are the numbers you asked for.'"

"Okay. Where were you yesterday?" I asked.

"Milwaukee."

"Doing what?" I pried.

"Customer delivery."

"What did you deliver?"

"A big piece of equipment that we built," he answered.

"How much did you sell it for?" I continued.

"$489,000."

Chapter Six – Finding Neutral

"And was this a repeat client?"

"Oh yeah," he said confidently. "They probably have 15 of our machines in their plant."

"How long have they been ordering equipment from you?"

"Since way before I worked here. At least 30 years."

"Okay." This was going to be easy.

I had been hired to help Al with his client interactions. The goal was to improve the number and size of his orders. Al was extremely talented as an engineer and plant manager. He just needed a little help saying things better to more people. This is where the PRNDL Process really helps. It's just a template. Once you can identify where in the process your client is, you know exactly what to say next.

"Write him back and say, 'Sorry I missed your call yesterday. We delivered a half million dollar piece of equipment to a 30 year client of ours and I wanted to be there personally to make sure there were no problems.' Then tell him, 'Here are the numbers you need.'"

The idea of a neutral third-party can come from anywhere. In this case, it bordered on being a testimonial, but facts are facts. The equipment cost half a million dollars and it was a 30 year old client. Those numbers are "neutral" because they are independent of the sale at hand.

Identifying neutral sources of authority is easy once you get started. Think of the last time you read an article or a trade journal or something and thought, "This is exactly why people should buy from us." That material should be repurposed to make the case for you.

Going back to my meeting with Tom, the Patriot's fan, I could see how important it was that the letter we sent our prospects had the name and amount of the mortgage on it. We were borrowing credibility from this neutral organization. I also realized how powerful it was to ask for a driver's license.

Update

When I took Doug's advice seriously, I had a calendar blocked out with dates and times for booking appointments, going on appointments, submitting applications and following up on applications. I still had not quit my job and I couldn't wait until I could. All my commission checks went into an account to help make the transition from a salary to 100% commission.

There's no doubt I was burning the candle at both ends. But I didn't consider it work. I love to work. I wasn't walking away from the job so much as I was walking away from an environment where no one gets awarded for outperforming their peers. From that standpoint, I was very competitive.

As I became more competitive and turned in more business, I started to get recognized. First, I started to stand out in Doug's group. I was second or third every week. Scott, Greg or Debbie would be ahead of me. We had weekly conference calls, so our names and sales numbers were announced for everyone to hear. This really leveled the playing field, unlike my current work situation where only a few people knew how much everyone else made. As we were selling, everything came to light. No one could hide from what the numbers showed.

"The numbers don't lie," Randy would say.

In addition to our team's conference call, we had a national conference call every week. Randy hosted that call. At any given time, there were 2,000 people on that call. And they announced the leaderboard top 20 for everyone to hear. Just before the call, they emailed the top 100 leaderboard to everyone. I read through that list, sizing up my competition. I was determined to make it onto the leaderboard and have them call out my name.

Reviewing the Steps

Things were really coming together for me. I had the script committed to memory and, like the case with Tom Brady's owner, I could adapt when I needed to.

More importantly, I had adapted these principles. First, highlighting that a prospect was not stuck in **PARK**. Next, I **REVERSED** things by demonstrating my concern for the prospect beyond the sale. And now I knew the importance of citing a **NEUTRAL** third party.

Radio and television commercials caught my attention more often, because I could see when they were using these techniques. But I still wanted to learn more about persuasion and influence. I had no idea then how much more there was to learn.

Rear View Mirror — What We Learned in Chapter Six

- We must present ourselves as the indifferent professional making a recommendation instead of a pushy salesperson with an agenda.
- The importance of citing a third-party that is recognized, verified, authorized, endorsed, or certified.
- See the Appendix for examples of using the third part of The PRNDL Process: **NEUTRAL.**

Chapter Six Exercises

1. How can you incorporate **NEUTRAL**, third party references in marketing material or sales scripts? Survey results of authorities? Professional endorsements? In what ways, or from which sources can you garner a distinction such as official, recommended, preferred, endorsed, rated, certified, licensed, authorized, credentialed, or commissioned?

_____

_____

_____

_____

_____

_____

2. Let's do some homework. Simply Google the terms "trends in [industry] in [current year]" or "what to expect in [industry] in [next year]" What statistics or trends support your solution to your competitor's' solution? Make sure to capture the source of those statistics.

_____

_____

_____

_____

3. Now, let's apply the homework we just did. What upcoming trends will make your solution more valuable or relevant in the future? What is happening in technology that will make your solution more valuable or relevant in the future? What is happening in population changes that will make your solution more valuable or relevant in the future? What is happening in financial markets, political climate, or legal environments that will make your solution more valuable or relevant in the future?

_____

_____

_____

_____

_____

7. USING LANDMARKS

Road Map — What We'll Learn in This Chapter
- How to identify a couple of high-level strategies people use when processing information.
- How knowing those strategies can help you influence your prospects' decisions.

Making Calls to Prospects

Making calls one night and going on appointments the next night became the norm. I was definitely ready to quit my job.

"Hello, Mr. Litton? Yes. This is Carl Brown. I'm calling about the letter you sent us."

Sometimes, people were courteous, "What letter?"

"About mortgage protection."

"Oh, that's right. I'm sorry."

And sometimes people were just rude.

"Hello, Mrs. Clive? This is Carl Brown with the Mortgage Protection Center. I'm calling about the letter you sent us."

"I didn't send you anything. I told you people to stop calling me." Click!

"But I haven't ever called you before, and your signature is on the letter we got," I said to myself after she hung up.

Sometimes people were completely clueless. Like the guy who set an appointment, welcomed me into his home, answered my first few questions and then said, "I thought you were calling about the reverse mortgage."

"What?" I wondered.

Then there were the people who just insulted my intelligence when I showed up at their house.

"No, I can't meet with you today. It's like I told the gal that called me. I'm busy today."

"I'm sorry. What gal did you talk with?" I asked, puzzled.

"The lady that called and booked the appointment." The sense of indignation was growing, even if it was completely contrived.

"But Mr. Hurley, I'm the one that talked to you on the phone," I wondered how far I should press it.

"No, you didn't. It was some woman," he answered.

"Sir, I called you yesterday at..." I looked at the top of the letter he sent in to us, "3:55. I asked what time would be good to meet and you said today at 6. Do you remember talking with me yesterday?"

That was an example of my pride getting the best of me.

But I couldn't help notice something about people between when I talked to them on the phone and when I met them in person.

For example, I might end my phone call like this, "Okay, Mr. Denis, 6PM it is. Again, my name is Carl Brown," I summarized.

And he might say, "Sounds good."

Or it might end like this, "All right, Ms. Waxman. Tomorrow at 7PM. And, again, my name is Carl Brown."

And she might say, "I'll see you then."

It took me a lot of phone calls before I started to notice the pattern. And the pattern would carry over into the appointment. Some said, "Sounds good," while others said, "See you then."

With Mr. Denis, I would finish a part of the script in the home and ask, "Is that about right?"

To which he would reply, "Yes, that sounds good."

Likewise, Ms. Waxman would respond in person the way she did on the phone. "Is that about right?" I would ask.

She responded with, "Yes. That looks about right."

Both of them were saying the same thing, but they were using different words to express it.

I started to pay careful attention to when and why someone would say it one way instead of the other. When I was on the phone with the prospects, I would write a word down if they used it twice, underline it if they used it three times and circle it if they used it four times. If my lead sheet had the word, "see" underlined and circled, then I would make sure to use that word in the appointment.

Connecting With Agents

And it happened with other agents as well. For example, I was on the phone with Doug one evening after a couple of appointments, and he said, "Hey, we need to change the dial-in number for our conference call tonight. I'll text these agents, but can you please text Debbie and Greg?"

"Sure," I replied. "No problem."

Then I sent the same message to Debbie and Greg.

<<Per Doug, tonight we will be on the new conference call line. Okay?>>

Debbie and Greg both replied at the same moment.

Greg's reply said, <<See you on the call.>>

Debbie's reply said, <<Talk to you then.>>

Now, arguably, there's not much difference if we're going to meet in person with a client. You can say, "See you then," or "Talk to you then." But with a conference call, it seemed like a stretch for me to think of it as "seeing someone" on the call.

Because this was coming up more and more, I decided to research it a bit.

That's when I learned a lot more about how our brains work.

Some people process information predominantly through what they hear while others predominantly visualize what they process in their mind. A small percentage are neither but are kinesthetic instead. They process through intense feelings.

What this means is that people who are visual need to formulate an image in their mind in order to move forward. By contrast, someone who is auditory is not looking for things to align, so much as they are listening for resonance or harmony— even with ideas.

Taken even further, this research was telling me that people who are visual can process information much more quickly than those who are auditory. What this meant was that I should probably slow down if I find myself talking with someone who is predominantly auditory, and it might help to draw a picture with people who are visual.

But sounds and sights were just the beginning of understanding all the different strategies and sorting methods that our brains use.

For example, after setting an appointment with prospects, they would usually try to give me directions. At first I didn't really listen because I was going to use a GPS anyway and I would probably not remember everything that the prospect said when I needed it.

But when I started listening to them giving directions, I was amazed at the different types of directions I would hear. Some people would give directions based on things that were "big."

For example, they would say, "Take a left turn at the big intersection," or "Look for the big sign," or "Go past the big house."

Others would give directions as if every restaurant was a well-known landmark. "Go past the Shoney's, then turn left at the Taco Bell."

The more I paid attention to the words my prospects used in casual conversation, the more I could relate to them when I used those same words.

Cross Traffic Does Not Stop

I loaded the kids up and we drove to the campground. I hadn't spent much time with them, and I missed them. Plus, I just needed to spend some time away from work. I needed a break.

We pulled up to a stop sign out in the country. Next to the stop sign was another sign that said, "Cross traffic does not stop."

Knowing that my kids would one day be driving, I decided to take this opportunity to teach them something.

My daughter was sitting next to me. So, I pointed out the sign to her. "Do you see that sign? It's very important when you see that sign to make sure and stop completely and check traffic both ways."

"Why, Dad?" she asked skeptically.

"Because you might think that because you're at a stop sign that traffic coming the other way will also stop."

Just then, a car whizzed by. "See?" I said. "Cross traffic does not stop."

Looking at her face, I could tell that she didn't understand what I was saying or why I was saying it.

"But it did stop. Why can't you just go?" She asked.

"No, they didn't stop." I was really confused by what she said. "They just drove right past us. Didn't you see them?"

"Well, yeah, Dad, but it's stopped now."

"What's stopped now?" I was very confused.

"The traffic. There isn't any."

Wow.

Right then I realized the ambiguity in the street sign's message. I read it and understood it to mean that the traffic that was going across our path did not have a stop sign; therefore, they would not be stopping. My daughter read it and thought it meant that the stream of traffic crossing our path would be relentless and never stop crossing our path.

As you read this, you might hurt a little between the ears. I don't understand why my daughter thought that, but it doesn't matter. She thought it. She interpreted the sign to say something that I couldn't have even imagined.

What I understood right then was that things might be black and white to me. They might sound perfectly clear. They might appear to be crystal clear to me. But the way I perceive them doesn't matter if I'm trying to communicate with someone else. What matters is that I understand the way my prospects perceive things.

If I were talking to someone who is predominantly auditory, then it would be a waste of time to use visual descriptions. Likewise if I was talking to someone who was visual, it would do little good to talk with auditory cues.

But understanding these differences was nowhere near as monumental as what I learned that day while camping with my kids.

Mis-matchers

We threw frisbee, climbed trees and stumps, threw a football, crossed an old obstacle course.

I let them play together for a while as I fixed our lunch. Then, I whistled for them to come over, and they all came running.

Katie was the oldest. She was a beautiful, responsible, compliant, smart young lady.

Luke was younger, but just as tall and already doing well in sports and school.

Grace came running behind them, laughing all the way. She was the outgoing one. The social butterfly. Talking a mile a minute. She sat down next to Luke.

Grace was wearing a red shirt and gray sweatpants. Luke was wearing a gray shirt and red sweatpants.

Grace looked at Luke's pants. Then she looked at her shirt. Then she looked at Luke.

"Luke! We match!" she said, as though she had just opened a Christmas present.

Chapter Seven – Using Landmarks

One look at Luke and I could read him like a book. This was my melancholic and contrary son. The sky could be clear and blue, and Luke would worry about when it would rain.

Before he could answer, I whispered to him, "I'll bet I know what you're thinking."

"What?" he asked. His face conveyed the skepticism and doubt he had.

I whispered, "You're thinking she's crazy for suggesting you guys match."

His skeptical frown turned to sheer amazement. "How did you know that?"

I knew that because I had come to know them. Pretty much anything anyone said, Luke would disagree with. No matter what you said, Grace would enthusiastically support it.

If there was one cloud in the sky near the horizon and behind a hill, you'd better not tell Luke that the sky is clear.

At the same time, if there was one spot of sky in an otherwise overcast, cloudy day, and you told Grace it was a clear day, she'd agree and point to the one spot where the clouds broke up.

I started to watch for this trait in others. If I suggested a business idea to my friend Mike, he would agree that the idea was worth millions. He'd recommend I file for a copyright, register the domain, and start on the idea as soon as possible. Meanwhile, if I told my friend Joe about the idea, he would frown, shake his head, and then list out thirty-seven ways this business idea would fail. Mike was a matcher. Joe was a mis-matcher.

Most engineers, lawyers, and accountants I knew generally seemed to have the "mis-matching" gene. Pretty much anything you said to them would get contradicted or shot down.

Among my adult friends, I noticed a way to identify whether someone was a matcher or a mis-matcher. Mis-matchers poked jokes at people they liked. It's a classic gambit for a mis-matcher to make fun of someone they like.

With my kids, I started testing an approach. With my mis-matching son, I would start out with a negative and let him turn things around. For example, I would start by saying, "I'm not sure this is right, but..." It worked like a charm on my son. I started trying it out on friends of mine who were engineers, accountants ,and lawyers. It didn't work all the time, so I looked for a way to identify whether someone was a matcher or a mis-matcher.

"What is the relationship between these three things?" I asked my friend as I laid three quarters in front of him.

"They're all quarters," he replied. "Is that what you mean?"

I tried it on another friend, "What is the relationship between these three things?"

"Two are heads up and one is tails up."

And another, "What is the relationship between these three things?"

"They're all round."

When I was in high school and college, I had teachers who asked their students to take different personality tests. You have probably taken one of these tests. If not, you probably know what I mean. The problem is that there are so many different possibilities. One test distinguishes 16 different personalities.

But this wasn't helpful to me in sales because either I didn't know what personality a prospect was, or if I did know, how could I remember which of the sixteen approaches I should use?

But now, I had added two tools to my toolbox. First, the auditory/ visual distinction. Secondly, the matcher/mis-matcher distinction.

If a prospect used words like "see," "look," and "bright," then I knew that prospect processed information visually. With these prospects, I would match vocabulary and rely on pictures to convey product features. I would also talk at a faster pace and convey "the big picture." On the other hand, with prospects that used words like "hear," or "listen," I would speak more slowly, and match vocabulary so that I could be "heard loud and clear."

Later, when I began doing sales and marketing consulting, I would always begin a relationship with a new client by placing three quarters in front of them and asking, "What is the relationship between these three things?"

The different replies I got never ceased to amaze me. Since the question is so open-ended, the answers vary greatly. I've had clients respond with, "They're all worth twenty-five cents." This answer is more consistent with a matcher, but notice that the focus is on monetary value.

Another client said, "They can get you either a piece of gum from a candy dispenser, or all together they can buy you a cup of coffee." This client was focused on the relative value of the coins and their usefulness. This is slightly different from the previous response.

I've had people say, "They're all round," or "They are all made of metal." No matter what the response is, it tells you the first area of focus that someone has. Value, shape, material property.

My favorite response was a client who looked at the quarters suspiciously and said, "They're not mine." This client literally didn't leave money on the table in his business dealings.

One client looked at the quarters and replied, "They're all quarters." Then after a brief moment, he leaned in, looked at the quarters, and reported every last detail of difference. Their orientation, the year they were minted, the state's name if it was listed, the distance between the left two and the right two.

Here's what I took from that interaction. With that client I always reported a brief, high-level summary, and then attached lengthy documents with all the supporting details. When I shared presentations with him, I always started with a summary page.

Then I showed him a list of supporting slides and gave him the chance to choose what details to look at.

One of the greatest sales teachers and coaches of all time, Harvey Mackay, required his sales team to find out and memorize sixty or seventy facts about each of their clients and prospects. I applaud his diligence and I recommend that strategy. But if you only have time to find out one thing about a prospect, show them three quarters and ask them, "What is the relationship between these three things?"

Giving Directions

My wife was going to join up with us at the campground after visiting with her sisters. Since this was before the days of having Maps and GPS on all cell phones, she had asked me to leave her directions to the campground.

"What's this?" she asked me, holding up the map I had drawn out.

"It's a map of how to get to the campground," I said, thinking this was some sort of trick question.

"I can't read this. I need directions." And the battle of the sexes was on.

Since the beginning of time, men refuse to stop and ask for directions, and apparently, this man was not capable of giving directions when asked.

"These are directions to the campground. See? Go west on 74, North on 256..."

"Carl, this doesn't help me. Which way is north?"

"Okay, let's think about this. In the morning, the sun will be behind you..."

Not sure what I was thinking... or if I was thinking. So, I made a little table with rows and columns.

Row #1: Take 74 for 34 miles, or about half an hour. Get off at the exit for 256 and turn right, or north.

Row #2: Take State Route 256 north for 8 miles, or about 15 minutes...

I even added a column for the approximate time she would arrive at each turn. Looking back, it's pretty funny because online Maps provide directions both ways: as a drawing and as a table.

But this is the main point. If we want to influence a decision, if we want to convince someone of something, we should be speaking the same language as our audience and using our audience's metaphors. If we are going to help someone arrive at a certain destination, we should give directions based on the landmarks used by our audience, regardless of what style we prefer.

Closing

So many things were coming together for me now. I followed my plan. The math worked. I followed the script. I was closing deals. The next thing I had to do was leave my job.

Although my boss probably didn't see it, it was really hard for me to do.

Our executive team was assembling for an impromptu meeting.

"Don't forget you need to get me those numbers, Carl." Christina reminded me as we sat down.

"Right. No problem," I assured her.

"Can we meet right after this meeting?" she asked.

"Absolutely," I said, knowing she was going to find out shortly that I was leaving.

"Okay, everyone, let's get started," my boss began. "Today's meeting will be really short because I know everyone's got stuff due, and I have another meeting to get to."

Everyone was fine with that. It seems like meetings only occur in one hour increments. Fortunately, this meeting was called in an unusual way. We didn't usually have impromptu meetings.

My boss continued, "Well, one thing that has been a constant in working together is the fact that things always change." Everyone was looking around at each other trying to figure out what we were going to hear.

"And today is no exception. Carl has decided it's time for him to leave and embark on another path. So, he'll be wrapping up some projects ,and the 12th will be his last day."

Everyone seemed to go through emotions of sadness, bewilderment, and resignation very quickly.

"So, let's wish him the best."

"Carl, what are you going to do?" two people asked in unison.

"I'm starting an insurance agency." Wow, it felt great to say that.

I was going to miss many of my coworkers, but as soon as everyone found out I was leaving, everyone made it easier. I'm not sure why anyone wants a two week notice. Meetings got rescheduled without me. People didn't seem that friendly. It was all a reminder that home is where the heart is.

"Did you still want to meet, Christina?" I asked as people were breaking up and heading back to their desks.

"Umm, no, that's okay. Hey, Scott!" she ran after someone else who could get her what she needed.

The best part of handing in my resignation came as a surprise. When I got back to my desk, I checked my email and saw the leaderboard. For the first time, my name was on the leaderboard.

Number 48: Carl Brown

I had leapfrogged the 90s, the 80s, the 70s, the 60s and the 50s.

Chapter Seven – Using Landmarks

This idea of being in the top 10 wasn't far-fetched now. But I really wanted to hit number one.

Running leads at night and on weekends was really cutting into my life. I had less time with my wife and kids. I hadn't worked out in several weeks. Looking back at that time, I realize I missed several news cycles. But I was being rewarded for my work and I was making progress. The sense of accomplishment was great.

Later on, I would bring some balance to my work life, but I still had a few lessons to learn about sales.

THE PRNDL PROCESS

Rear View Mirror — What We Learned in Chapter Seven
- How to distinguish between people who process information visually vs auditorily.
- How to distinguish between people who are matchers vs mis-matchers.
- How to adapt our script or presentation depending on the strategy of our audience.

Chapter Seven Exercises

1. Thinking about your main client, or your boss, or even a spouse, are they more visual or auditory? (A very small percentage will be kinesthetic, but may appear similar to auditory.)

2. Thinking about the person from Exercise #1 above, try placing three quarters in front of them and asking, "What is the relationship between these three things?" What did they notice first? Second?

3. Are they a matcher or mis-matcher?

Access these worksheets and other resources at
Shift to High Gear.com
105

4. How do the answers to these questions change the way you talk to that person?

_____

_____

_____

_____

5. How can you change your script to find the strategy used by your prospect?

_____

_____

_____

_____

Access these worksheets and other resources at
Shift to High Gear.com
106

8. WHAT DRIVES OTHERS

Road Map — What We'll Learn in This Chapter
- How to leverage what *DRIVES* others.

Think About It

"We'd like some time to think about it."

The death of the sale. Think about it? What does that mean?

Do people sit around on a Saturday night and think about all the things they couldn't commit to during the week? When will you think about it? How will you think about it?

We were stuck. Somehow, I got stuck in the middle of the script.

"Okay, Crystal. I understand. But you and Marcus both said this was important to you."

"It is," she reassured me. "It's just that, well, I'm not sure right now."

We had gone through the script. I told them I assumed they cared about each other. They said yes and then explained why.

I told them I couldn't get them approved, but that I could help complete the application and submit it with a check for the first year's premium. They understood.

They told me why they sent the letter in to us. They wanted to have coverage, but they also liked the idea of getting their premiums back at the end of their coverage.

Then, when I explained how the coverage worked, it seemed like they were on board. But when I told them how much it cost, we got stuck. And we stayed stuck for a long time.

Normally my appointments were just under an hour, but we were now past 90 minutes and going nowhere.

My mind was on my next appointment that started in 45 minutes. I was on a roll this week, and I was on track to break into the top 20 on the Leaderboard. I really wanted to get out of there, but I also really wanted two checks from them.

"Focus," I told myself. "When you're with a prospect, be present to the prospect." I fought the urge to think about my next appointment.

"Is it a matter of the price?" I asked. "Were you expecting it to be lower?"

"It's not that."

"Because one option for you is to get the coverage in place by itself without the return of premium. That would bring the price down, but still allow you to protect your house should anything happen to you."

"Yeah, but…"

"But what?" I thought.

"…but then we'd lose all those premiums," she said.

"But you'd have the coverage in place, at a rate lower than coverage with the return of premium."

"What do think?" she asked her husband, who seemed just as anxious as me to get this appointment over with.

"I don't... whatever you think is best," he deferred to her. Great. Should I just leave?

I asked to use the bathroom, which I hoped would give them time to talk. But when I came back, we were still stuck.

Return of premium was an innovative feature. It increased the monthly premium by a bit, but at the end of the term, 100% of the premiums were paid back to the policyholder. And since that money had already been taxed, it will be paid back tax-free.

Could you just invest the difference in a mutual fund and get a better return? Maybe... if you knew which mutual fund would outperform the market. But it wasn't a question of investing the difference. In order to compare apples to apples, you had to consider that the difference invested would only pay dividends on the amount invested, not the full premium.

The best valuation was to compare the two options. The first option involved paying X for life insurance, and at the end of the term, you'd get back X plus Y (the cost of the return on premium rider). The second option involved paying X for life insurance and investing Y. At the end of the term, you'd have Y plus growth. And since the premium for the life insurance was less than the cost of the rider, that growth after taxes had to be mighty big to make up the difference.

It wasn't a very complicated concept, but it took some explaining. In either case, Crystal and Marcus (or maybe just Crystal) were stuck. Should they or shouldn't they?

For some reason, I opened my mouth and said something I had heard on one of the conference calls. It wasn't scripted, it wasn't rehearsed, it wasn't planned. Heck, if I had planned it, it might not have worked.

"One thing more and more people are doing is getting 20 years of coverage with the Return of Premium rider. That way, in 20 years, they'll get a lump sum paid out tax free and they can apply it to their mortgage and pay it off early."

"Then we wouldn't need to worry about the coverage, would we Marcus?" she looked at her husband, whose face revealed that he was no longer listening to our discussion.

I wanted to say something, but I could tell that what I said had impacted her dramatically enough that I didn't want to stop her.

"He's saying that most people get 20 years of coverage with this rider on it, and then use it to pay off what's left of their mortgage." He leaned his elbow on the table and covered his mouth with his fist.

Well, I had not said, "most people," but again, I was not about to get in her way.

"Would that really cover what's left of the mortgage?" she asked.

I ran the calculation and showed that, yes, it would cover the majority of what was left on their mortgage.

Crystal reached out and pulled the application closer to her. Later I would learn that both his and her actions were buying signals. Covering his mouth with his hand, touching the product (in this case the application), talking about the future as if they had purchased the product. These were all buying signals.

"Would you feel good about applying for it that way?" I asked.

"Yes," she said, enthusiastically.

After I filled out the application, collected their checks and put my laptop away, she said again, "I'm really glad that you told us that most people our age are getting the 20 years of coverage instead."

Once again, I didn't want to argue with her. But it was amazing. She used the word, "most" when I had said, "more and more." And she said, "people our age," when I had never said anything like that. Either way, she felt much better about these options than she felt about the first option I showed her.

I drove to my next appointment. And like I've said before, the best time to make a sale is right after you make a sale.

The Leaderboard

The next morning, I recounted the whole thing to Doug.

"Man, I just wanted to get out of there," I complained.

"Why? Just because it was taking some of your time?" Doug asked. "You're going to make over $1,000 and you're bummed that it took you more than 60 minutes to do it?"

"Well, I'm just saying that it was going nowhere." I tried to defend myself.

"Right, but, when you're with a prospect…"

"I know, be present to them. I even said that to myself when I was in the meeting."

"Okay," he conceded, "But don't forget that the client is the reason we're doing this. You can't expect everyone to throw money into your basket just because you drove out to their house. You have to earn it."

"You're right. You're right."

"But you know what you did that was awesome?" he asked with a smile on his face. I was on the phone with him, but I could tell that he was smiling because of the sound the 's' made. When an 's' whistles, you know that it comes from a smile.

"What?" I asked, smiling back.

"You not only listen to the conference calls, but you put into practice the things that you hear on the calls." I didn't have the heart to tell him that what I said came out unintentionally. "And you were using social proof. That's a huge factor of influence."

"What?"

"Social proof. You know, you told them that other people were doing a 20 year policy with the rider." He paused. "Aw, c'mon, don't tell me you missed that?"

I had very nearly missed it.

"People want to be individuals, just like everyone else." We both laughed. "She was probably sitting there thinking, 'How do I know this is a good deal? This guy is going to tell me it is a good deal, but that's his job.' But when you told her that other people are using this as a financial strategy, it made her feel confident that she was making a good decision and not losing her shirt."

Looking back, he was exactly right. She didn't want to say, 'No,' but she wanted confirmation that this was not a stupid idea.

"Social proof is huge," Doug reaffirmed. "It's like, ***what DRIVES others*** drives us. We want to wear what's trendy. We want to eat in restaurants that have a long wait. We want to know what the best-selling cars are. We are social creatures, and what our peers do influences us."

He was right.

"It's why we use testimonials when we're recruiting other agents."

That's when I realized how much of ***what DRIVES others*** was used on me as a writing agent.

- Conference calls
- Leaderboards
- Guest speakers on the conference calls
- Testimonials

In fact, the reason I even brought up a 20-year solution to my client Crystal and her husband Marcus was because I had heard another agent on a conference call sharing some of the things he said to prospects.

"But Carl!" Doug changed topics. "Are you at your computer?"

"No, why?" I asked.

"Aw, man! You've got to get on your computer!" He sounded like he was going to explode from enthusiasm.

"What is it?" I asked.

"I'm not telling. But are you going to be on the national call?" he asked.

"Yes."

"Okay. Then we better get off the phone!"

He definitely had my curiosity. I ran to my computer while I got ready to dial-in to the conference call.

There it was. The Leaderboard.

Carl Brown- #18

I had broken into the top 20. That meant that they would announce my name on the conference call.

Examples of *What Drives Others*

For the next several days, I could see examples of *what DRIVES others* (or social proof) being used everywhere I went.

- The number of reviews on Amazon helped me choose between two similar products.
- My wife and I were trying to choose between two restaurants, and we went to the one with more cars in the parking lot.
- In order to find a gift for a friend, I looked at the New York Times Bestseller List.

- An old McDonald's restaurant still had a sign out front listing, "billions and billions served."
- A popular television show reminds potential viewers of their Nielsen ratings.
- A billboard for a local university showed pictures of students from a local high school with the caption, "Students from (this high school) attend (this university)."

Social proof has exploded with social media. Companies now live and die by their Yelp and Google reviews. Companies list logos of their clients on their websites.

The term "Social Proof" didn't exactly fit into my "PRNDL" mnemonic. I have placed it under "D" for *what **D**rives others*." And "social proof" didn't find a place in the formal version of the script we used. But it came in handy when trying to put someone over the top on making a decision.

Reviewing the Steps

By now, I was making sure to cover several steps in every meeting.

First, I made sure to identify how a prospect was not stuck in **PARK**. And I verbalized the ways they were not in park to them.

Next, I **REVERSED** things by demonstrating my concern for the prospect beyond the sale. I made sure they knew how much I cared, not just how much I knew.

As a third step, I now knew the importance of citing a **NEUTRAL** third party and I did so whenever I could.

Now, I added in another tool. I made sure to highlight *what DRIVES others*.

Rear View Mirror — What We Learned in Chapter Eight
- The value of knowing what *DRIVES* our prospects' peers.
- Examples of what *DRIVES* others.
- See the Appendix for examples of using the fourth part of The PRNDL Process: *DRIVE.*

Chapter Eight Exercises

1. Identify ways that you can incorporate client testimonials into your script or messaging.

_____

_____

_____

_____

_____

_____

2. Let's do some more homework. Identify a composite profile of the biggest groups of clients you serve. What do you know about them? Age, Demographic, Educational Experience, Budget, Industry, etc. Enlist the help of your marketing department or your IT department to help you do some analysis.

3. Give a name to the two or three groups of clients you have in order to characterize their needs.

Group A

_____

Group B

_____

4. Identify why that group of clients buys from you, and what about their decision is different from other groups.

Group A

_____

_____

Group B

_____

_____

5. Write some examples of how you can use this distinction in your script. "Most people like you are looking for ____, or they end up buying ____."

Group A

_____

_____

Group B

_____

_____

Access these worksheets and other resources at
Shift to High Gear.com
116

9. TURN BY TURN

Road Map — What We'll Learn in This Chapter
- What a roadmap for success is and how to identify yours.

Jim's Roadmap for Success

"So, how are you doing, Jim?" I asked.

"Awesome," he said, with a plastic smile that tried to mask the depression he was experiencing.

Jim was a very successful software developer. He had played college basketball at the University of Cincinnati, followed by two seasons for a professional team. Then, he went on to start a software company. He made several million dollars a year from residual income alone. But something wasn't going right.

"Awesome is good, right?" I asked.

"Awesome is very good," he lied, as he sipped on his overpriced coffee.

Chapter Nine – Turn by Turn

"So what's really going on?" I asked, as I sipped my cheap water.

Panera was the go-to place to meet someone to just talk. Me? I was living the low-carb life, so no pastries for me. And coffee? I can't stand it. So, Panera with a glass a water is a common thing for me.

We had struck up a conversation one day while waiting for our kids' soccer game to end. Once he learned that I was in sales, we started talking about that, and then he asked if we could meet for breakfast at Panera sometime.

"I don't know. I'm just in a rut these days," he said.

I waited for him to share more by keeping my mouth shut.

"And I keep thinking I'll snap out of it, but I don't. And I just keep staying in this rut."

I sipped my water to help me keep my mouth shut.

"But everyone gets stuck once in a while, right?" he asked, and took another sip of his steaming hot coffee. "How do you get out of a rut, Carl?"

"That's a good question, isn't it?" I said. "It's really THE question for us in our professional lives, isn't it? And maybe our personal lives, too, right?" I talked as though I was an expert.

"Yeah, maybe, but I'm just talking about my professional life," he confessed.

"Okay, what's going on?" I asked.

"Well, I used to just drive, drive, drive. I was relentless. I didn't stop. I saw a goal, and I pursued it until I achieved it. And lately, I've been... I dunno."

"Stuck?" I asked.

"More than stuck. Some days I have a hard time getting out of bed."

Jim was describing a "funk." We all get stuck sometimes. Call it a mental block, a slump, stage fright, writer's block, whatever you want. Everyone experiences something like this at some point.

But the number one rule of business is to stay in business. This means that regardless of what business model or industry we're in, sustainability is essential. And if we're self-employed, and everyone who sells is self-employed, sustainability is all a matter of keeping your spirits up and persevering.

Ironically, mental blocks show us the importance of willpower and mind over matter more effectively than anything else.

"Wow—getting out of bed?" I asked. "That's serious!"

"I know."

"I was listening to this motivational tape the other day and it sort of made me laugh. The guy said, 'If you get stuck, just ask yourself, are you dumb or lazy? Do you not know how to do your work? If you know how, but you aren't doing it, then ask yourself why you aren't doing your work?'"

"Oh, I want to get out of this rut," he replied.

"So, do you know what you need to do?"

"Well, I know how to write software. I just haven't developed anything lately."

"Okay, this is a little different, isn't it? You're saying that you know how to solve problems or answer questions, but right now you need to know how to ask the right question. Is that about right?"

"Yeah, I guess so," he answered.

"Okay, well let's go back. Let's talk about something completely different. Let's talk about basketball. We'll see what we can learn from that, and then come back to talking about your current situation. Is that okay?" I asked.

"Sure," he said.

"Okay, because you were pretty good at basketball, right?"

"Yep," he sounded more confident with that short answer already.

"Okay, can you think of one of your biggest games?" I asked.

"Yeah, that's easy."

"Okay," I continued. "How did you prepare for that game?"

"Well, I practiced."

"Right, but I mean, what about the way you prepared for that game made it different? When you were in the locker room, was there music playing? Did your coach say something inspiring? What sticks out in your mind about preparing in the locker room?"

"It was quiet," he said right away.

"Quiet?" I asked.

"Yes. Nobody was talking. I remember just sitting there thinking about the game."

"Okay, good." I said. "What were you thinking? Were you thinking about how much you wanted to win? Were you thinking how much you wanted the other team to lose? Were you thinking about winning a trophy? Were you thinking about what someone was going to say if you won or lost?" I just hit him with a dozen questions.

"No, I just thought about what I needed to do in the game."

"Okay, good. Were you thinking about what you needed to do overall, or specific plays?" This was getting interesting.

"I was thinking about specific plays. And I thought about facing off against my man."

"When you were visualizing it, were you seeing yourself in the picture, or were you seeing the picture through your own eyes?" I asked.

Jim now had a far-off look about him as though he were seeing something as he looked through me. "Through my own eyes."

Summarizing, I reviewed what he had shared. "Okay, you were visualizing what you needed to do specifically when you were facing your man. Right?"

"Yes."

"Did you envision either of the coaches at all?"

"No."

"Fans?"

"No."

"Anybody else?"

"No."

"As you visualized this, did anyone say anything to you? Did you say anything to your man?"

"No. I just said 'Yes!' to myself after I made the shot."

"Okay, so you faced off with your man, you made a move, you beat him, and made the shot. Then you said 'Yes!' to yourself?"

"That's right."

"Okay, now let's talk about something else. When you began writing your first software program, what did that look like?"

"Well, at first, I brainstormed software solutions to specific problems."

Chapter Nine – Turn by Turn

"Okay, how? Did you type it up?" I asked.

"No, I just brainstormed in my head." He said.

"Okay. Where were you when you did that?" I asked.

"Well, I used to go bike riding."

"Really?" I was a little surprised.

"Yeah, I used to go for long bike rides."

"Who did you go with?" I asked.

"Just by myself."

"Okay, once you brainstormed a solution, did you identify all of the components and everything that needed to be done?"

"Yes."

"Did you write it down, type it out, or what?" I asked.

"I diagramed it on a white board," he said.

"Okay, cool. So, when you were identifying the components, did you focus on the overall program or just specific components?" This whole discussion was fascinating. I was getting a glimpse into the way he thought and the way he processed information.

"Specific components."

"Okay, did anyone track your progress? I don't know the answer here, Jim, but did you start out self-employed or did you work for someone?" I asked.

"I worked for myself."

"Okay, so, how did you… Wait. Did you, by the way, say, 'Yes!' to yourself after writing a module of software?"

"Hmmm," he said.

"What?" I asked.

"I say, 'Yes,' to myself after completing everything. Just like with basketball."

"Okay," I said. "That is significant. This is the pattern. You brainstorm the big picture, then you diagram the specifics. Then you visualize yourself solving a problem, running a play, etc. This happens in quiet solitude. Then, when you execute, you celebrate by letting out a 'Yes!'"

By now, the pattern had become very obvious.

"So, Jim," I began. "I can see a couple different important things to check. First, my guess is that you don't go for long bike rides anymore."

"That's right," he confirmed.

"So, you don't have quiet solitude to brainstorm ideas, do you?"

"No. No, I don't," he said, realizing the connection. "Sounds like I should, doesn't it?"

"Absolutely, Jim. You've had great success when you set your mind to it. And that success comes from quiet solitude to brainstorm everything out in your mind. Then, you diagram the specific components. Hey, wait a minute," I stopped.

"What?" he asked.

"Where did your basketball coach draw out plays?"

"On a whiteboard," he answered.

"It's pretty uncanny, isn't it?" I asked. "You follow the same path when you pursue success, even in totally different areas of your life. It shouldn't be surprising, but unless we take a step back, out of the way, we could have missed that detail."

He took another sip of coffee, so I drank some more water.

"So what about now? Are you going to start biking again?" I asked.

"No."

"Okay, so then what can you do that is similar?" I asked.

"I've got it!" he said with a snap of his fingers. "I'll just go back to taking long drives in the countryside. I started doing that when I stopped biking, but I haven't kept it up. Driving in the country really relaxes me and helps me think."

"Sounds like you've got a game plan." I was excited to see the results. When we finished breakfast, I asked him to, at the end of the year, calculate how much our conversation was worth to him based on new revenue.

My Roadmap for Success

Because I had learned to pay such careful attention to whether people were auditory or visual and whether they were matchers or mis-matchers, I realized that one person's roadmap for success was probably not the same as another person's. I helped Jim identify his roadmap for achieving success, so I decided to figure out what mine was.

I started by identifying my successes. What were they? I had not worked long, so I didn't have a lot to go on. But when I was in college, I planned, organized, and managed a bike race fundraiser. It was a huge job, took a lot of work, and it was a huge success. Plus, I maintained a 4.0 gpa that semester.

What other successes had I accomplished? I led our fraternity to become the #1 organization on campus—an award given by our student government association. This was fueled by my fierce rivalry with another fraternity.

Additionally, as a freelance sub-contractor, I had experienced several successful projects for a growing marketing firm.

By reviewing the elements involved in those successes, I was amazed to find that I had followed almost the exact same steps to achieve my goals each time.

They were:

1.) Someone told me that I couldn't be successful.
2.) I pictured what a successful outcome would look and feel like.
3.) Next, I made a calendar of upcoming weeks and identified everything that needed to happen in order for me to achieve what I had envisioned.
4.) I told myself in various convincing ways that I could indeed achieve the outcome.

This was my "forumula for success." Since then, I've read many other templates for success. Many of them are good. Many of them share elements of the roadmap I identified by looking at my track record. I think the key for adapting a roadmap for success is to evaluate what has worked in the past for *each individual,* and to pay attention to the sequence of the elements.

One thing that is very important is to look at each ingredient in the roadmap for success and identify what it is and what it is not. For example, the first step of my roadmap is that someone told me that I couldn't be successful. Here are the unique qualities of that step:

A.) It was **someone else**. It wasn't me.
B.) They **told** me. They didn't show me.
C.) They said I **couldn't** be successful. They didn't say I **could be** successful.

Some other distinctions could be colors, sounds, size, perspective, positives/negatives, big pictures/details. It's important to analyze each step thoroughly. That's where all the benefit of this process comes from.

Maybe all you need to do to change your motivation is to "tell yourself" you can do it instead of visualizing it. Or maybe you need to imagine someone else telling you that you can't do it, rather than imagining someone encouraging you.

Spend a lot of time making sure these distinctions are correct.

For example, in my roadmap it's crucial that I hear someone else tell me that I can't be successful. It really doesn't work if someone assures me that success will be easy. Also, for some reason, the color red plays a prominent role in my roadmap for success, not blue and not green.

For someone else, seeing a trophy might be the first step. Listening to a particular song might be another step. Having someone give you a high-five might be important. Explore as many distinctions as possible.

Getting Cocky

After reviewing my roadmap for success, I got pretty cocky. I must have thought I was a hot shot. I looked at my weekly schedule. I was booking appointments three days a week, and running appointments three days a week. For the most part, it went like this:

> Monday- make calls
> Tuesday- run appointments
> Wednesday- make calls
> Thursday- run appointments
> Friday- make calls
> Saturday- run appointments

It got pretty tricky though trying to make calls on Friday nights. That's when I had the idea to switch it like this:

> Sunday- make calls
> Monday- run appointments
> Tuesday- make calls
> Wednesday- run appointments
> Thursday- make calls
> Friday- run appointments

Sunday calls were easier to make because I could get it all done in a couple of hours at night. But either way, I missed spending time with my family.

That's when I decided to make calls in the morning. That looked like this:

> Monday morning- make calls for Tuesday night
> Tuesday morning- make calls for Wednesday night
> Tuesday night- run appointments
> Wednesday morning- make calls for Thursday night
> Wednesday night- run appointments
> Thursday night- run appointments

This worked really well, and it gave me Friday, Saturday, and Sunday off.

The only problem was that I had to deliver policies in addition to running appointments. So, I came up with a brilliant idea that proved to be disastrous.

Rear View Mirror — What We Learned in Chapter Nine
- Everyone has a Roadmap for Success.
- Not everyone's Roadmap for Success is the same.
- By reviewing our past successes, we can identify the key ingredients to our success, and we can duplicate our results.

Chapter Nine Exercises

1. Identify three professional successes you've had that were
   dependent upon your actions.

Success #1-

_____

Success #2-

_____

Success #3-

_____

2. Identify what steps you took to achieve those successes.

_____

_____

_____

_____

_____

_____

3. Pay attention to details. Did you hear something? See
   something? Feel something? Were those experienced
   externally or internally? Were they positive (do/can/
   should) or negative (don't/can't/shouldn't)? Was a
   sound associated? Colors? Specific people (spouse,
   child, parent, competitor)? Did **you** say or do
   something? Was something said or shown to you?
   Elaborate on the details. Even if it seems small, you
   won't notice patterns if you don't include lots of details
   first.

Access these worksheets and other resources at
Shift to High Gear.com
128

_____

_____

_____

_____

4. Review the sequence of the steps. Make sure you have the
   steps in the right order.

1.) _____

2.) _____

3.) _____

4.) _____

5.) _____

6.) _____

7.) _____

8.) _____

9.) _____

10.) _____

Access these worksheets and other resources at
Shift to High Gear.com
129

5. How can you recreate that sequence again and apply it to your current goals?

_____

2.) _____

3.) _____

4.) _____

5.) _____

6.) _____

7.) _____

8.) _____

9.) _____

10.) _____

Access these worksheets and other resources at
Shift to High Gear.com
130

10. LOW GEAR

Road Map — What We'll Learn in This Chapter
- How putting things in Low Gear can help cement a deal or close a sale.
- What happens when we don't account for the fact that people want what they can't have.

Cancellations

"Are you Carl?" She asked me through the screen door.

"Yes. That's me."

"Come on in," she held the door open. "Sorry for the mess."

"Oh, no problem," I reassured her.

A late afternoon appointment was not very common, but welcome. It helped me fit more appointments in the evening. Linda was a younger woman with two small children in a modest home.

"Linda, do you mind if I plug my laptop in here?" I asked. Little questions like that gave me the opportunity to test close, and I wanted to address her with her name as often as possible.

"Oh sure, that's fine," she said.

Pulling the lead from my briefcase, I asked, "Is this the letter you sent to us?"

"It sure is," she answered.

"OK. I assume that there's someone you care about that you want to make sure is taken care of in case anything happens to you. Is that right?"

"Yes," she answered. "My daughters."

The appointment was going like clockwork. She was friendly and receptive. She didn't flinch when I told her the price. I asked her for her driver's license. I started filling out the application. Everything was going smoothly.

"OK. Have I taken good care of you tonight?" I asked.

"Yes! Thank you."

"OK, what will happen next is that in a couple of weeks, when they approve your policy, they will send it out by mail. All you need to do is sign stating that you have received the policy. Does that make sense?"

"Yes," she answered.

I stood up, got my laptop, shook her hand, and walked to the door. "It was nice to meet you."

"Yes. Thanks," she said.

I put her application on the back seat and drove to my next appointment.

"Maybe I should stop at Taco Bell," I thought to myself. I knew the area well enough that I didn't need to look it up on the GPS.

As I sat in the parking lot eating my Chalupa, my cell phone rang. I did not recognize the number, but it was from the area code I was in, so I decided to answer the phone.

"This is Carl."

"Hi Carl, this is Linda. We just met about the mortgage protection."

"Yes?" I asked somewhat nervously.

"I decided against that. Please don't submit my application."

I didn't really respond at all.

"Can you tear up my check?" She asked.

"Ummm. OK, is something wrong?" I tried to think of what I could do to save the sale.

"No, nothing is wrong. I just changed my mind. Please tear up the check. Bye," she finished, before I could respond.

What the heck happened?

Was I obligated to submit her application? If I did not turn in the application, how would that impact my numbers? If the insurance company didn't approve her before she canceled, then I wouldn't get a chargeback. If I hadn't answered the phone, would I have submitted her application before I found out that she wanted to cancel?

Lots of thoughts were going through my mind.

The best time to make a sale is right after you've made a sale. So, the worst time to go on a sales appointment must be right after a cancellation. I did my best to put this out of my mind.

I drove to my next appointment. Karen greeted me at the door.

Chapter Ten – Low Gear

"Karen?"

"Yes, you must be Carl. Please come in."

Karen was also young – in her early 30's. It looked like she was a single mother. Her house was spotless. Her kitchen was newly cleaned.

"Would you like something to drink?"

"Yes please. Could I have a glass of water?" I didn't really want anything to drink, but this gave me a chance to thank my prospect for something.

"Sure. No problem," she said.

"Great. Thanks." She handed me a clean glass with ice water in it. "Thank you." I took a sip. "Okay. Is this the letter you sent to us?"

"Yes it is," she answered.

"OK. I assume that there's someone you care about that you want to make sure is taken care of in case anything happens to you. Is that right?"

"Yes," she answered. "Kylie and Sophia."

And so, another application got completed. Heart attack? Stroke? COPD? No. No. No.

It was very typical. The only thing that was different was that she knew her driver's license number.

"OK, Karen. Here's what will happen. In a couple of weeks, when they approve your policy, they will send it out by mail. All you need to do is sign a form saying that you received the policy and then mail the form back. Okay?"

"Okay," she said as her eyes squinted just ever so slightly. I would later learn from studying body language that this was not a good sign. And I didn't feel great about it at the time, but I thought everything was taken care of.

Plus, I wanted to get out of there and go home. So, I kept my manners and said goodbye to all.

Home was 35 minutes away, so I had time to think.

About 20 minutes after I had left, the phone rang.

"What is it now?" I wondered.

I waited.

Oh, what the heck? You can't lose something you never had. And I did not yet have a commission for the sale.

"This is Carl," I answered.

"Hi – is this Carl with the mortgage protection?"

Is there another?

"Yes," I said, summoning a sweet, cheerful disposition.

"This is Karen from over on Beckett Road. "

"Yes. Hi Karen. What can I do for you?"

"Well, I thought about it, and I don't want to go through with that application. Can you please mail it back to me?"

This time I had a better sense of what to say. "I'm sorry, Karen. I left you with a conditional receipt. You have conditional coverage in place right now. If something happened to you and someone found that receipt, they could file a claim. I need to submit the application."

"That's ridiculous," she said.

"Do you remember my explaining the conditional receipt?"

"Yes. But don't I get a certain number of days to think it over?"

"You can send a letter either to me or to the insurance company and let them know that you want to cancel the application. Their address is on the conditional receipt. You'll get a full refund. But if you want to cancel it, that's what you'll need to do."

I was a little annoyed, but I think I was still professional and polite.

"Oh, that's ridiculous!" She hung up on me.

Her phone call was not really that important to me. What was important was figuring out why I was losing business.

In the previous month, I submitted 35 applications. This month, so far, I had written 29 applications, but I had only submitted 15 to the insurance companies.

What was wrong? Was I losing my mind?

Something had to be different. But I didn't know what it was. So, I started reviewing everything in my mind again.

S.O.S. Call

"Doug?" I asked in panic mode.

"Hey Carl." He could tell I was panicking. "You have good news or bad news?"

Wow. Okay, that made me want to say I had good news. But that wasn't true. I was in full-blown freak-out mode.

"Bad news, I'm afraid. Doug, I've written 29 applications so far this month…"

He interrupted, "That's great, Carl! Keep it up and you're going to hit all your goals."

"No, it's not great. I mean, it would be. But of those 29 applications, I've had fourteen of them cancel on me. Fourteen!

That's almost half! What am I doing wrong?"

"Calm down. One bad week doesn't make a bad month," he tried to reassure me.

"Right, but this is a bad month now."

"Okay, but one bad month doesn't make a bad year," he tried again.

"Doug! I've got bills to pay. I need to make money! The more clients that cancel, the less money I have. I'm screwed!"

"Carl, calm down. Have you changed anything? Are you using the script?" he asked.

"Yes, I'm using the script. No, I haven't changed anything."

"Okay, well, I am hosting the conference call here in 15 minutes, so, let's talk about this after the call, okay?"

"Okay," I lied. It wasn't okay. How could I make ends meet? This was a disaster!

Under the Bridge

I still remember exactly where I was on the road when the next thought entered my mind. I was just about to go under a highway overpass in downtown. That's when I thought to myself...

"With so few policies issued, I'll have plenty of time to deliver them."

That's when the light bulb went off in my head. That's what had changed!

I had gotten so cocky and so arrogant that I didn't want to have to deliver the policy to my clients. But not only had I decided not to deliver the policy; I had decided to tell them that the policy would be delivered to them. This went against the whole idea that I was on their side, helping them to get approved by the insurance company since I couldn't approve their application.

It all started to make sense now. I was telling the prospect that I was on their side. I was trying to use the *"**REVERSE**"* step and show them how much I cared. But then, after I got them to write a check, I was telling them that they would get a policy delivered, and I was giving them instructions on what to do when they got the policy.

In my mind, I could hear Randy saying on a national conference call that, "People want what they can't have." By telling them that I couldn't approve the policy, but that I had to submit the first month's payment, I was showing them that I cared. I was impartial. I was here whether I got paid or not. I was on their side. But I was betraying all that with my closing comments. No wonder they called me right away to cancel! They must have thought I was a jerk! And a liar!

And, what's worse is that it was true. My drive for efficiency drove me to saying things that conflicted with each other.

I couldn't believe how one simple line could change so much. As I drove out of downtown, I saw a couple of billboards. They understood this concept and conveyed the same message. "Limited Time Only," "Prize for the First 500 in Attendance," "Registration Opens on…"

All of these messages conveyed urgency. Either the product was in short supply, the window of time to buy it was in short supply, or the staff was hard-pressed to help so many people who wanted to get the product. Low inventory. Low supply. Limited time. Lost opportunity possible.

This became the "L" in PRNDL. It's obviously an important step, and it falls last in the sequence because it is the call to action. "Low supply." I could now see how all of the other steps led to this step.

This step called the prospect to action for fear of losing out.

Take Away City

Randy was so right. "People want what they can't have." And here I was, pretending that my prospects couldn't get coverage, and then telling them that coverage was inevitable. My mixed messaging was destroying my business.

I remember Randy saying on a conference call one time, "If they start to look disinterested, then it's take-away city."

It's an odd expression, right? "Take-away-city?" This refers to a technique that is often referred to as the "take away."

The "take-away" is the opposite of a pushy salesperson. In some ways it's a bit of a reversal. Some salespeople script this step by saying something like, "I'm not sure that I'm the best person to help you," or "We might not be the right fit for you."

In this way, the "low supply" step or "take away" appeals to the mis-matcher. The mis-matcher hears someone say, "This isn't right for you," and the mis-matcher responds with, "I will prove you wrong!"

Well, I knew enough now to know that I never, ever, ever wanted to repeat this problem again. That's when I added a couple of lines to my script. The first time I included these lines were VERY uncomfortable, but nothing like the discomfort of having half of my applications get canceled before I turned them in.

Reviewing the Steps

Here's how my next appointment went with a woman by the name of Penny:

Point out that she isn't in "Park"
- Is this the letter you sent in to us?
- Okay, well, I assume that you care about somebody and that you want to make sure that if anything happens to you, they will be taken care of.

Test Close
- Is that right?

Keep showing her that she isn't in "Park"
- Okay, so, what about this letter made you send it in to us?

Reverse Things
- Now, I can't get you approved for this coverage.
- What I can do is explain how this coverage works. Then, we can submit an application with the first month's premium to see if we can get it approved.

Test Close
- Does that make sense?

Finding NEUTRAL
- Can I see your driver's license?
- What's your Social Security Number?

Demonstrate what DRIVES Others
- What I see a lot of my clients doing is...

Then I kick it into LOW gear
Once I had a completed the application with a check for the first month's premium, I turned the check around to Penny and asked her, "Here's the coverage we're applying for. Is this right? {pause} Okay, is it right for *you*? Because here's what I don't want to happen: I don't want you to get 1 month or 3 months or 12 months down the road, and have you call me and cancel because this doesn't meet your needs. Because if it doesn't meet your needs, then I would just say, 'Take the check back,' because you and I are both wasting our time."

Closing

The good news is that after that abysmal month was over, I went right back to a high level of production. The next month, I turned in 32 applications, and I never had any prospect take the check back at that point, or cancel an application after that.

Just a couple of weeks after turning things around from all of the cancellations, I opened my email and dialed in to the national conference call to find at the top of the Leaderboard:

Carl Brown #1

Rear View Mirror — What We Learned in Chapter Ten

- How easily we can mess up a great script by veering from The PRNDL Process.
- People want what they can't have.
- See the Appendix for examples of using the fifth part of The PRNDL Process: **Low Gear.**

Chapter Ten Exercises

1. Thinking back to previous sales you've closed, what finally moved the prospect to buy? Was it the end of a quarter? Was it a sales incentive? Was it low inventory?

\
\
\
\

2. From observation of previous sales, what can you do for or say to other prospects to create a sense of urgency in order to close the deal? [See the Appendix for examples of using the fifth part of The PRNDL Process: **Low Gear.**]

\
\
\
\

PUTTING IT ALL TOGETHER

Using your answers to the end of the chapter exercises, let's construct a script using The PRNDL Process. (Also see the APPENDIX for examples of each step.)

Step One- *PARK*

What can you say to prospects to leverage their past behavior or things they've said that demonstrate they are not "in *PARK*" in order to "steer" them towards a purchase?

\
\
\
\

Step Two- *REVERSE*

What can you do for or say to prospects to demonstrate your willingness to put them first?

\
\
\
\

Access these worksheets and other resources at
Shift to High Gear.com
142

Step Three- *NEUTRAL*
How can you incorporate *NEUTRAL*, third party references that support your case for the prospect buying your solution?

_____

_____

_____

_____

Step Four- *DRIVE*
How can you incorporate client testimonials into your script or messaging?

_____

_____

_____

_____

Step Five- *LOW* GEAR
What can you do for or say to other prospects to create a sense of urgency in order to close the deal?

_____

_____

_____

_____

Access these worksheets and other resources at
Shift to High Gear.com

EXAMPLES

(A) Business email original

This is an actual example of a before and after email message where I applied the PRNDL Process. This was sent to me by a client looking for feedback as I was finishing my book. The details have been masked.

Here's the original:

Mr. Smith,

My name is Carl Brown and I am a Senior Consultant with Acme Consulting. Julia Foley asked me to follow-up with you to discuss [our program] and its implementation at [your company]. I work with both the certifications and with the on-site workshops. I hope to talk with you next week regarding how we can assist you in increasing [KRAs] through [our program] – I witness it happening everyday with great companies like yours that choose to make this investment.

I can be reached at 866-555-1212 anytime (if I am in a session, I will return the call ASAP).

Carl Brown

(A) Business email with edits:

Mr. Smith,

Julia Foley asked me to follow-up with you about increasing [KRAs] at [your company].

I just left you a voice mail, and I wanted to follow-up by email. At this point, it would be good to hear your perspective on the areas that you think have the most opportunity for improvement.

Next week, I'll be running a workshop in [city], but I can schedule some time on Tuesday morning or Wednesday afternoon.

Which works better for you?

-Carl Brown

Here are some notes about how I applied The PRNDL Process:

(**PARK**) By citing Julia Foley, this reminds the prospect that he's not in park.

(**REVERSE**) By showing that the phone call is connected to an email, diligence is being demonstrated. This shows that the prospect is not being pursued impersonally.

(**NEUTRAL**) By showing that a workshop is coming up, we're showing the prospect that we're busy and a limited resource that is in demand. This fact is neutral and doesn't contribute to sales pressure.

(**DRIVE**) The fact that a workshop is being held next week also shows that peers are benefiting from this work.

(**LOW Gear**) By showing the prospect that time is limited and by giving him two options to choose from, we demonstrate that our services are in demand. We also take command of the calendar and offer a choice between two positive outcomes instead of asking a yes/no question.

(B) EMPLOYEE BONUS PROGRAM

A business owner I know had a bonus program in place for his employees. He wanted to impress upon his employees the value of the bonus. By creating this incentive, his employees provided better customer support. In return, they were eligible for a generous bonus program every three months.

He walked to the front of the conference room where all of his employees were seated.

He said, "Raise your hand if you have benefited from the bonus program. "

Examples

This showed everyone that they were not in *PARK*. They were already a part of the bonus program.

Next he said, "This quarter $20,000 is going towards the bonus program. That money could have been spent by me on a vacation home in Florida."

This was his way of *REVERSING* things. He was showing what he was sacrificing for their benefit.
Then he said, "I tell other businessman about our bonus program, and they think I'm crazy."

With this statement, he was citing a *NEUTRAL* third-party. And he was emphasizing to his employees how he had *REVERSED* things in their favor.

Then he gave one example of how the bonus program has benefited one of the employees. This was the fourth step of the PRNDL process. He used a testimonial to show that the bonus *DRIVES* others.

Finally, he called everyone to action by telling them what they needed to do and when they needed to do it by in order to qualify for the bonus program. He shifted into *low gear.*

(C) FUNDRAISING

Revenue from our "Fall Banquet" fundraiser at our school was barely enough to cover the cost of the event. We hosted a dinner for thirty tables of ten people each. We had dinner, listened to a guest speaker and then made an appeal. One year I made the ask. Here are the steps we took to improve on our return.

PARK- I asked all the teachers to stand and pointed out that they all worked as a sacrifice for the school. Then I asked all the parents who paid tuition to stand and pointed out the sacrifice they made when the alternative was a free education at a public school. Then I asked everyone who had ever donated time or money to the school to stand and then I thanked everyone. From here on out, I was able to refer to "us" as stakeholders.

REVERSE- I pointed out to everyone that thanks to careful preplanning and the generosity of a couple people and a corporate sponsor, the entire evening was already paid-for. No one had to buy their dinner. Everyone was a stakeholder, but truly a guest for the evening. Then I highlighted the value of listening to the guest speaker. So everyone knew that the dinner and entertainment for the evening had already been provided.

NEUTRAL- Because we planned ahead of time, the guest speaker spoke well of our school community and especially the results of our students. I cited that in order to demonstrate that neutral third-parties recognized and valued what we were accomplishing.

DRIVE- We shared the personal story of members of the community who benefited from tuition assistance in order to build the case for supporting out tuition-assistance program.

LOW- We held the event close to the end of the year, so we used the deadline for counting a gift as tax-deductible as the incentive for making a gift right now.

A couple other things contributed to our success. Instead of referencing the tangible ways a gift helped the school, we referenced the personal benefits. For example, I've heard fundraising appeals such as, "Your gift of $100 keeps the lights on for a week." Instead, we personalized it to our students and to families in our community.

And I've found that when it comes to charitable giving, it's easier to visualize the benefit to one person than it is to visualize the benefits to a group of people. One scholarship is easy to grasp. Feeding all the hungry of the world seems overwhelming, and is impersonal at the very best.

For that reason, we had students come to each table with envelopes to collect the gifts. Each envelope had the picture of a student along with a handwritten message from the student thanking the donor in advance. By thanking the donors in advance, we were "getting them out of **PARK**." And by personalizing the ask, we were also putting things in **REVERSE**.

Another key to our success was personalizing the ask. Rather than

Examples

asking everyone to give a certain amount of money, I asked everyone to visualize a number specific to them. Here's what I said, "I want you to visualize something. Either you experience this or your spouse shares this story with you. It's late on a Friday afternoon and your boss comes in your office. If you're self-employed, visualize your accountant coming in. It's been a busy week, but a good week. And it's been a good year for that matter. There have been fires to put out for sure. And there have been difficult people to deal with. But your late afternoon guest has good news. You're not going to believe it. Your hard work has paid off. Revenue is unexpectedly up and that means a bonus dividends for you. You call your spouse to share the news. How much are we talking about? What kind of unexpected bonus or dividends would be worth calling your spouse to talk about? I don't know what that dollar amount is. Is it $500? Is it $5,000? Or maybe $10,000 or more. Whatever that unexpected bonus is, I want you to consider making a gift of that size."

When we looked at the results, we increased our net revenue by 40% and each year afterward maintained the higher level, rather than falling back down to the previous average.

(D) SELLING JEWELRY

As I was finishing this book, I found myself at a party with three former jewelry sales people. One of them heard that I had written a book on sales and that the title had the word, "process" in it.

I could see in her eyes right away that she was skeptical. "Do you think sales is a *process?*" she asked.

Since she had been very successful in sales, I asked her what the secret to her success was.

"Romance," was her first answer. "Ask them about their relationship. How did they meet? What was their courtship like? How did they know they were meant for each other? Get them talking about the proposal. That sort of thing."

To me, this was no more than getting the couple out of **PARK**.

Next, she said that she would bring her manager into the equation by trying to get a better deal for the client. To me, this seemed *a little* like finding a **NEUTRAL** third party. But it was the next thing she said that was brilliant.

"After talking to my manager and getting a lower price, I would offer to cover the sales tax if they bought that night."

This **REVERSED** things AND put them in **LOW** gear. She was putting herself on the same side as the buyer and giving them a reason to act now.

Yes. I think you can apply a process to sales.

(E) CAR WASH

I had the opportunity to share The PRNDL Process with a group of highschoolers as part of a literature/persuasive writing class. After I explained each of the steps in the process, I had them script a message to the community, encouraging them to come to the annual car wash. The car wash was unique, because it was not a fundraiser. It was a service project. It was one of many service projects the school did every month.

The final script looked like this:

"For the past 10 years, you have participated in our car wash. (Get out of **PARK!**) This car wash is one of many service projects that we do every month that provides over 5,000 hours of service to the community every year. (Put things in **REVERSE!**) While the typical car wash charges money or asks for a donation, we are not accepting donations, but instead are doing a car wash for free. (With nothing to gain, the message itself is **NEUTRAL.**) We will be washing cars on Tuesday and Wednesday from 10 AM until 2 PM only." (Hurry up, because our availability is limited and in **LOW** supply.)

(F) MOM AND DAD, BUY ME A CAR!

I worked with the high school students to develop another script for something else. I asked them to write a script to use with their parents so that their parents would buy them a car.

Examples

The final version looked like this:

1st line: "Mom and Dad, when did you get your first car?"

(This got their parents to open up. By talking about when they got their first car, it got them out of **PARK** by showing that they had their first car at some point. This helped lay the groundwork for their parents at least matching the timeframe for getting the first car.)

2nd line: "If I had my own car, I could make trips to the grocery store for you, or take my brothers and sisters to and from practice for their sports."

(This **REVERSED** things, and showed the parents what's in it for them.)

3rd line: I encouraged the students to find statistics that demonstrated the benefits of high school students having a car.

(These statistics would be **NEUTRAL**. Examples could have been, "Students with their own cars learn responsibility," or "Students with their own cars end up being safer drivers in the long run." With on-line search engines, there are plenty of opportunities to find and cite statistics in favor of teens having their own car.)

4th line: Name a family whose children have their own cars.

(This shows what **DRIVES** their peers. I made sure to specify that they pick a family that their parents respect. Then they can say, "so-and-so bought their kids a car." One point of clarification. The students wanted to say that their friend had a car. But the focus should be on the peer *of their parents*, not their own peers. Citing their friends as peers could backfire. Instead, they should appeal to the parent and use their peers as examples for social proof.)

5th line: "Right now, there's a great deal on a car at this car dealer."

(Shifting into **LOW** gear in this case involved some more research as well. If they did a little homework, they could recommend that their parents buy a specific car. They could show that such and such a car, with a Kelley Blue Book value of X is available for sale at a dealership or online, and then emphasize that that car which is a good deal, won't last long.)

RECOMMEND READING

We can learn through experience or through reading.

I recommend asking everyone you know who is successful what books they recommend for professional development.

Below are the books that have been recommended to me that have had the most impact on my career.

They are listed alphabetically.

Awaken the Giant Within, Tony Robbins

Five Minutes with VITO, David Mattson and Anthony Parinello

Influence: The Psychology of Influence, Robert Cialdini, Ph.D.

Never Split the Difference, Chris Voss

Presenting to Win, Jerry Weissman

Selling to Big Companies, Jill Konrath

Words that Work, Dr. Frank Luntz

ACKNOWLEDGMENTS

First and foremost, I want to thank my wife Amy. Everything I do is thanks to her and because of her. She's the greatest person I've ever met and my best friend.

I also want to thank my amazing Mom.

Thanks to my kids, especially to Katie and Luke for proofing my manuscript.

Andrea Ferraro and Beth Dobrozsi both provided great feedback on my manuscript. And they were great teachers to my kids. Thank you, both!

Thanks to my brother, Drew who helped keep me on track with my writing.

Professionally, I have had the pleasure of knowing, working with and learning from many talented people.
I must mention Tony Ferraro first. Collaborating with him has been the highlight of my career so far.

I also want to thank Tim Bete, Lori Turner and Fran Evans. I have learned so much from the three of you. You are among the most talented professionals I know.

The **Shift to High Gear Sales System**© is based on maximizing what we think, say, and do.

In order to get motivated, stay motivated and keep your mind sharp, Carl is preparing to introduce "**Fuel-Up Your Sales**" with 10 motivational strategies to increase sales.

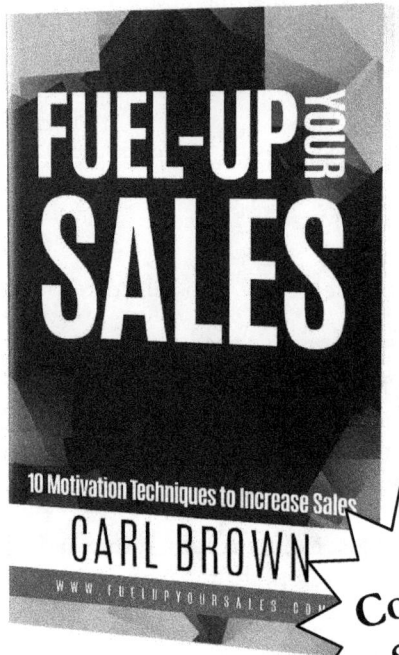

The **Shift to High Gear Sales System**© is based on maximizing what we think, say, and do.

In order to be productive and get more done, Carl has developed "Tune-Up Your Sales" with productivity techniques to increase sales.

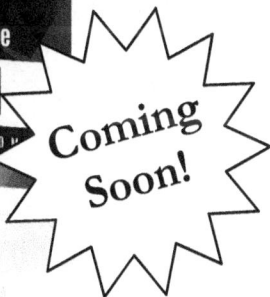

Register at **Shift to High Gear.com** for updates on new releases and to access free resources!

The **Shift to High Gear Sales System**© is based on maximizing what we think, say, and do.

The PRNDL Process is one way to quickly improve your sales message. But to improve every aspect of your sales process from prospecting, to overcoming objections, to productivity tips and recommendations on technological tools, Carl offers a three-day training system with 6 class segments each day. This is the most cost-effective way to get your sales team producing at the next level.

Go to **Shift to High Gear.com** to check availability and to access other resources on-line.

ABOUT THE AUTHOR

Carl is a husband, father and sales & marketing consultant, in that order. He has helped both for profit and non profit organizations increase their revenue by millions of dollars.

After an undergraduate degree and an MBA, Carl spent 10 years at a Midwest university where his data analytics helped exceed a $150 million fundraising campaign. It was during those years that Carl began studying influence.

Carl started an insurance agency where PRNDL continued to evolve. But when he started a sales and marketing consulting firm, his work with dozens of clients across the country allowed him to fine tune PRNDL and its execution. Carl's experience as President of the Board of Directors of a private school even allowed him to test The PRNDL Process with a non-profit that launched a high school to complement the existing PreK-8th grades.

Carl has been asked by many clients to come work for them but his most important professional goal is helping others reach their potential by sharing The PRNDL Process.

His most important personal goal is making homemade ice cream and sourdough pizza for his family every Sunday night.

You can reach Carl at: Carl.Brown@ShiftToHighGear.com

The PRNDL Process is available at bulk pricing!

Make this resource available to your entire sales team.

This book is perfect for your sales team.

- **Story format** makes it **easy to read!**
- **Chapters are topical,** so it's **informative!**
- **Content is biographical,** so it's **proven!**
- **Summaries, exercises & templates** make it **easy to implement!**

Volume	Pricing	Discount
1-9	$14.99	0%
10-24	$10.00	33%
25-50	$8.00	46%
50+	$6.00	60%

For bulk pricing, email orders@shifttohighgear.com.

Register at **Shift to High Gear.com** for updates on new releases and to access free resources!

www.ingramcontent.com/pod-product-compliance
Lightning Source LLC
Chambersburg PA
CBHW050507210326
41521CB00011B/2356